# Who Called
# The Police?

# Who Called The Police?

**Real Police.  Real Drama.  Real Funny.**

# D.R. Novak

authorHOUSE®

AuthorHouse™
1663 Liberty Drive
Bloomington, IN 47403
www.authorhouse.com
Phone: 1-800-839-8640

Published by AuthorHouse   05/10/2013

ISBN: 978-1-4817-5193-3 (sc)
ISBN: 978-1-4817-5192-6 (e)

In memory of Michael and Bernice . . .

# INTRODUCTION

Welcome to police work. I've been a big city cop for twenty years. My partners name is Sam. Sam and I were high school buddies and came on the job at the same time. We thought that joining the police force would be an excellent career move: arresting criminals, helping people, becoming well respected in the community—boy were we wrong.

We started our career the same way all recruits do. We took a written test (multiple guess quiz) followed by medical tests (turn your head and cough), then a physical agility test (being able to run without falling down), a psychological test (that was the one that worried me) and finished by passing a drug screening test (thankfully they don't test for alcohol) and, lastly, a background check (no skeletons in the closet).

Having passed all these hurdles, Sam and I were sent to the academy for intensive training in criminal law, use of non-lethal force and firearms training. Our class size consisted of 40 recruits of all shapes and sizes—and I mean all shapes and sizes. One recruit was about 6 feet 7 inches in height (think basketball center) and one woman was 4 feet 9 inches (they eventually had to make a special squad car for her with block pedals so she could reach the gas and brake pedal).

While the class size started out at forty, it didn't end there. About ten weeks into our training the department threw a surprise drug test. Apparently one recruit did a little celebrating after being hired and tested positive for marijuana. Oh well, better to weed out (pun intended) the drug users early.

A second classmate was also fired fourteen weeks into training. During this week of classes, we were sent to the computer lab for training. The instructor randomly picked a recruit as an example of how to properly run a person's name for outstanding warrants and criminal histories. When the instructor put the recruits name and birth date in the computer database, a warrant popped up on the computer screen for robbery. The instructor tugged at his collar, let out a nervous laughter and proclaimed "something must be wrong with the computer." The class was quickly dismissed for lunch, and when we returned Internal Affairs was leading the recruit out the door in handcuffs. Let's just say, being fired wasn't his main concern at that point.

After graduating from the academy, Sam and I were sent to different Districts for street training. For six weeks, I was assigned a Field Training Officer (FTO). During that period my only job was to follow my FTO around and learn how things are really done. During that period I refrained from smashing up the squad car or shooting myself, which means I passed with flying colors. I was now certified by the State as a Police Officer.

Sam and I immediately put in a transfer to the 33rd District so we could be partners. Now the 33rd District isn't exactly what one might call the Gold Coast of districts. Requesting a transfer to a District is based upon seniority, something we had very little of. This was the best we could do.

Some districts are called 'retirement districts' because crime is low and a tour of duty is a piece of cake, and some districts are called 'fast districts' because of the high crime rate and heavy demand for police service. Based upon this criteria, the 33rd District should be called 'supersonic.' But here is where our illustrious careers embarked. While the names have been changed to protect the guilty, after all, they are the ones with all the rights, this book is a chronicle of true stories I have come across as a police officer. The stories are tilted toward the humorous side because if there's one thing I learned as the police—you better have a sense of humor.

So why did I write this book? Well, one day my partner looked at me and said, "you can't make this stuff up, someone should write a book about this."

# CHAPTER 1

## The Purse Snatch

Roll call ended at 4:15 p.m. It was Friday and that meant get your running shoes on because it was going to be busy. My partner, Sam, got our portable radios and car keys and we headed for the squad car. I use the term "squad car" loosely since the car had over 200,000 miles on it and squeaked and creaked like it was haunted. But no respectable ghost would consider haunting a scrap of metal like this. In fact, our car was dubbed the Fred Flintstone car. Why? Because the floor where the driver sat was rusted out, leaving a hole the size of a sewer cover. As you drove, you could look down and see the pavement rush by. And, if the brakes ever failed (which is by no means a long shot), I could press my feet down and stop the car like Fred Flintstone did (in this department using the term "preventive maintenance" could get you in trouble with the labor unions).

As I settled behind the wheel and peered through the windshield with several spider cracks, my partner nestled into the passenger seat, which isn't easy with his burly frame. While Sam wasn't that tall, about 5 feet 8 inches, he was built like a fire plug—thick arms and legs and 180 pounds of muscle. (Sam was the brawn and I was the brains—relatively speaking). Before I could start the car the radio began to crackle. Just our luck, we were first up tonight.

The dispatcher announced, "beat 3322"

We ignored her at first hoping she would move on to someone else for the moment so we could get our usual cup of coffee before running from call to call. The dispatchers knew the routine of that first cup of coffee out of roll call and would hold calls for a few minutes. The fact that she didn't this time meant it was probably urgent.

I answered up, "beat 3322, go ahead dispatch."

"Beat 3322, see the elderly woman injured during a purse snatch, 11844 S. Green Street."

The cup of coffee would have to wait. Sam and I could pick up a coffee on the way, but that wouldn't be fair to Manny, the owner of the local eatery on the beat. Manny always gave us free coffee, with one stipulation: We had to sit in the diner and drink the coffee. For the ten minutes we sat in the diner with the squad car parked in front was the best security for the establishment (of course that only works for the ten minutes while we're there, the diner was robbed twice in the last month).

I proceeded directly to our call and as I rounded the corner of 119th Street and Green I could see the address we were looking for. It was a small, one-story medical facility. No one was waiting in front, so I parked the car and Sam and I went inside.

A nurse in a white uniform was waiting at the door. She looked upset and escorted Sam and I to a patient waiting area where an elderly woman was sitting in the corner by herself. The lady looked like she was pushing seventy, no more than eighty pounds, with thinning grey hair and a trusty cane be her side.

The nurse spoke first: "Officers, this lady was coming to see a doctor when she was accosted by a man outside . . . right in broad day light!"

As I looked closely at the elderly lady, I noticed a small bruise on her forehead and several scratches on her right arm. I crouched down to be eye-level with the woman and asked in soft voice, "what happened?" The lady remained silent. I looked up at Sam who shrugged his shoulders. I paused for a moment and then took a seat next to the lady. I leaned toward her and stated, "Ma'am I want to help, but you have to tell me what happened."

The lady took a deep breath, turned toward me and stated, "I got out of a cab . . . I was walking to the front door when a man appeared out of nowhere. The man grabbed my arm and yanked at the purse in my hand. I tried to hold on, but I couldn't. As he pulled on the purse I lost my balance and fell to the ground. I think I hit my head on the pavement."

It is things like this that really tick me off. This poor woman, a poster-child for all grandmothers, was minding her own business when a thug decides, let me take what I can from the most vulnerable members of society, she won't be able to defend herself.

But I kept my composure, and stated in my most reassuring voice, "well, at least you're in good hands here, a doctor can check out that noggin. Can you give me a description of the person who did this?"

The lady thought for a moment, than replied, "It happened so fast, all I can remember is that he had on a red shirt."

Sam reached into his coat pocket and retrieved a police report. He started to ask the lady several questions, "what's your name?"

"Rose" was the reply.

"O.K. Rose, can you tell what was in the purse?

Rose looked down and did not reply.

Sam asked again, "Rose, I need to know what was in the purse for the report, in case we later find the contents so we can return the property."

Rose looked up and mumbled something unintelligible.

Sam looked at me for help, but I had no idea what she said either. Thinking I might have better luck I stated, "Rose, you're going to have speak up."

Rose lifted her eyes, carefully scanned the room for a moment and whispered, "I was coming to see a doctor . . . a doctor who needed a sample to analyze. I was bringing him a sample. That's all that was in the purse."

Feeling lost I replied, "I don't understand Rose, can you be more specific.

"It was a sample for the doctor, in a plastic sandwich bag . . . it was a . . . a . . . a stool sample."

Now I know it's my job to act in professional manner, especially with a victim of a crime present, but I felt an urgent need to laugh. Not a giggle under your breath type of laugh, but a bellicose, gut-wrenching laugh. I turned to my partner for support and found him racing for the door, his face crimson red and his cheeks swelled to twice their size. Apparently I wasn't the only one who saw the humor in this. I wanted to run from the room also, but I thought to myself this lady was robbed and sustained several injuries, the last thing she needs is insult to injury with the police who came to help her laughing at her.

After several deep breaths, and I mean several, I was able to compose myself, looked Rose straight in the eye and said, "let me get this straight, some guy stole your purse and the only thing in the purse was a turd?"

With a sense of relief on her face, Rose nodded up and down.

I excused myself from the room and headed for the door. As I exited the building, there was Sam sitting at the curb looking like he was having a seizure from laughing so hard. What could I do, other than join him.

After getting that out of our systems, I headed for the squad car while yelling at Sam, "get in."

Sam hopped in the car and looked at me with a puzzled expression. He asked, "where are we going?"

"We handled enough purse snatches in our day, what does an offender do after stealing a purse?" I could see by Sam's expression, he had connected the dots.

While criminals are dumb, they are not stupid. When a criminal steals a purse, the first course of action is to rifle through the purse and take anything of value, usually money, and discard the personal items and the purse. The offender knows if the police are close and he is stopped, the thief can deny the theft and he has no incriminating evidence on him, other than money, which is not traceable back to the victim.

As I drove up and down side streets heading in the direction of the downtown area of the city, thinking this guy might be searching for a place to wash his hands, Sam spoke, "But partner, even if we find a guy with a red shirt, how are we going to prove it's the same guy who stole the purse.?"

I smiled at Sam, "it's not the red shirt that's going to give him away, instead of using your eyes, use your nose." As I completed the sentence, Sam pointed at a man walking hurriedly down the sidewalk. He had his right hand tucked in his pants pocket; he was wearing a red shirt. I pulled the squad car up onto the sidewalk blocking his path.

Sam jumped from the car and grabbed the man by the shirt. I exited the car and raced around the vehicle to assist. Sam told the man to put his hands on the squad car and not make any sudden moves. The man put his left hand on the car but kept his right hand in his pocket. Sam ordered the man to place both hands on the car. Usually when someone refuses to obey a police order to show his hands, it means the person is concealing a weapon. But somehow I already knew he wasn't concealing a weapon, he had an ulterior motive. Reluctantly, and slowly, the man eased his right hand from his pocket and placed it on the squad car. That's when it hit. The stench was overwhelming. I took a step back as my eyes began to tear up. Sam looked like he was ready to vomit. It was then we realized we had our man, the turd bandit.

Taking a few more steps back and trying to get upwind, I told Sam, "put some handcuffs of him."

Sam shook his head at me, "you handcuff him."

Ut-oh ! While I was pleased with myself for assuming the offender, while fleeing the scene, reached into the purse searching for money and got crap all over his hand, I didn't think what to do if we found him. I didn't want that on my handcuffs, and I certainly didn't want to put him in the squad car.

"Listen Sam," I said, "technically you jumped out of the car and grabbed him, so he's your prisoner."

'Nice try," Sam countered "but it was your idea to look for him and your smarts that assumed he would smell when we found him, so you can take credit for the arrest, and you handcuff him."

I glanced over at the offender and noticed a smirk on his face. He was probably thinking he was going to walk away from this. After all, he did have us. If Sam or I weren't going to handcuff him, he would be free to go.

I turned my attention to the offender and yelled "catch" as I threw the handcuffs at the offender. The offender caught the handcuffs with a befuddled look. I ordered him, "handcuff yourself."

The offender took one cuff, placed it over his wrist and clicked the cuff till it tightened. He then placed his hands behind his back and repeated the process on his other wrist. I guess, technically, he arrested himself.

Sam immediately started to interrogate the prisoner, "where's the purse at?"

Now, usually, this is where you get the song and dance routine form the prisoner about how you got the wrong guy and I'm innocent. But he knew he was caught red-handed, or in this case poop-handed. He knew he did it. I knew he did it. Everyone standing down-wind knew he did it.

He gave a full confession, including the alley where, after sticking his hand in the purse, he threw the purse in a garbage can.

Sam put the prisoner in the back seat of the car while I rolled down all the windows. Back tracking to the alley with the garbage can, I opened the can—big mistake. The pungent aroma that was released from that confined space hit me like a punch in the face. I quickly shut the lid.

Sam laughed under his breath and asked, "now what?"

"Well, the way I see it, the prisoner confessed so we really don't need the purse as evidence in court. And, I'm sure the old lady is not going to want a purse back that's smeared with feces". So I looked at Sam with a devious smile and replied, "what purse, I didn't see any purse.

Sam concurred, "whatever you say partner."

It was short drive back to the medical facility. Sam went inside and escorted the elderly lady back to the squad car to see if she could identify the offender. While the prisoner did confess to the crime, there's always the chance when he gets to court (and smells a lot better) he might change his story.

"O.K. Ma'am," Sam asked, "is this the guy who stole your purse?" She peered through the window at the prisoner. A blank stare came across her face.

Not to worry I thought. I motioned for Sam to have the elderly lady move closer to the car and have her lean in. As she hugged the door of the car and leaned in, I could see the aroma hit her face. Her knees started to buckle and Sam put his arm around her support. "That's Him," she declared."

Sam looked in my direction and stated, "shit happens."

# CHAPTER 2

## The Funeral

It was a Saturday afternoon and Sam and I finished our lunch (yes, it was free for the police) when the Sergeant got on the radio and asked to meet us.

Our Sergeant was in his late 50's and getting close to retirement; or, as he like to say, "I retired years ago, the department just doesn't know it yet." After 30 years on the job, the daily stress, along with eating on the go (mostly fast food) and gravity took a toll on his body. He was easily 250 pounds with a belly that drooped several inches below his waistline. And with a full head of curly white hair, he could give Santa Claus a run for his money. But Sam and I had a good working relationship with our Sergeant—we never saw him on the street. We would see him at the beginning of our tour at roll-call, and at the end of tour when we were leaving. That was it, and that suited us fine. Nobody wants their boss looking over their shoulder while they are working. He knew how we worked (bending the rules on occasion) but he trusted us enough to know we would get the job done and would not do anything to embarrass him—too much.

So it came as a surprise when the Sergeant got on the radio and asked to meet us in a vacant lot on our beat. On the ride over there, Sam turned serious and asked "what did we do wrong this time?"

I began racking my brain thinking of what we did. The sergeant didn't say anything to us at roll-call, I thought to myself, so it must have been something within the last four hours. I was coming up empty.

Every call today was routine, and every citizen seemed happy with our service. I can't picture anyone wanting to complain.

I told Sam, "I got nothing." How can we get our story straight and come up with a good excuse when we did nothing wrong?

Sam pulled the squad car into the vacant lot where the Sergeant was parked with his window down. He pulled alongside the Sergeant's car and rolled down the window. "What's up," my partner enquired, while squirming back and forth in his seat.

Sensing Sam's apprehension, the Sergeant smiled, "relax guys, no one is beefing (complaining), I have a special assignment for you. Remember, a few days ago when that gang member was killed on your beat standing on the corner?"

"How could we forget," I replied. After all, while the victim was only 21 years of age, he was a high-ranking member of a local street gang. That day a car drove by and unloaded several shots from a semi-automatic pistol into his body (the detectives on the scene recovered 44 shell casings from the crime scene). And, as usual, nobody saw it. The detectives canvassed the neighborhood (knocked on the doors of everyone within a block radius of the crime) and got the standard reply: 'I don't want to get involved."

"Well," the Sergeant continued, "the wake is going on right now. I don't expect trouble, but I need a squad car to stay at the funeral home until the wake is over."

"And by someone, you mean us?" Sam asked.

"Thanks for volunteering," the sergeant quickly said while shifting his car into gear and pulling off before we could reply.

"Great," Sam mumbled "now we have to baby sit a group of gangbanging mourners."

I wasn't too happy either. But I knew a squad car at the wake wasn't a bad idea. It's usually mandatory for every gang member to show up to pay their respects or they get violated (breaking the rules of the gang resulting in some time of punishment—usually a beating at the hands of your fellow gang members.)

Reluctantly, Sam drove toward the wake. The funeral home was a white building located in the middle of the block. Two Roman columns flanked both sides of the entrance and supported a roof extending from the building to the street. Under the roof was a narrow driveway used as a portico for the hearse. The hearse was jet black with chrome-spoke wheels and smoked (dark tint) windows. In short, the hearse was a rolling traffic violation. The windows, for one, violated several city ordinances. The dark tint prevented anyone approaching the vehicle from seeing inside—a clear danger to law enforcement officers approaching a vehicle and outlawed in our State. But, hey, who's going to stop a hearse and write tickets.

Sam decided to park the squad car directly in front of the funeral home and do some people watching. The clientele streaming into the wake was not encouraging—mostly young males that Sam and I have encountered before. Now when I say encounter, I mean arrested. So Sam and I decided to play a game of 'what's my line' (an old game show where a guest would appear and several contestants would have to guess his occupation).

Sam went first. "The guy with the blue t-shirt walking in, we locked him up in a stolen auto—he's an auto thief."

My turn. "The guy wearing a green jacket, we locked him up twice with packets of cocaine—he a drug dealer."

Sam pressed on. "The lady with the red dress, we locked her up for soliciting just last week—she's a prostitute."

"No fair," I protested, "that's only a misdemeanor, I thought we were doing felonies."

Sam sighed. We knew it was time to get serious. The Sergeant wanted us to make our presence felt, which meant getting out of the car and going inside. I got out of the squad car and headed for the front door with Sam right behind me. Sam and I side-stepped the metal detector (yes, the funeral home has a metal detector you have to walk through to get in. In this neighborhood everyone has a metal detector, including the secondary and elementary schools, and the store-front churches). We entered the small lobby and stepped on some shag carpeting that had the 1970's written all over it. Directly ahead was a small desk with a line forming—several people were waiting to sign the guest book.

Sam leaned over and whispered in my ear, "I wonder how many of these mourners are signing with aliases?"

I poked Sam in disapproval. "Don't make me laugh in here. We could start a riot."

Behind the desk was a long hallway that funneled into the viewing room. Here, several rows of folding chairs were facing the casket. The casket was blue, with gold trim across the edges and matched the gold handles (I'm sure that was just a coincidence, since those are the two colors that represent the gang). To the right of the casket were an abundance of fresh flowers and funeral wreaths. Standing directly in front of the casket was a very young woman (she looked like she should be at a Senior Prom, not a funeral). She was wearing a black pants suit and something about her face seemed odd. My guess was she was the girlfriend of the deceased (notice I didn't say wife. Not many couples partake in the bonds of holy matrimony in this neck of the woods. Besides, government assistance checks are bigger if your single).

Sam and I stood at the back of the room trying to look somber. A room full of gang members and police just didn't mix. It was a toss-up as to who was more uncomfortable—the mourners who occasionally glanced at our presence with cold stares, or Sam and I, doing our best imitation of trying to look respectful.

After about an hour this, a man in a dark suit, apparently the funeral director, approached the front of the room and started handing out white gloves to several mourners to act as pall-bearers.

Hoping that the wake was about to conclude, Sam and I backed down the hallway and took a position in the lobby. As I gazed out the front door a man had opened the back door of the hearse to receive the casket. None too soon, I thought to myself, and we'll be out of here. As the mourners started streaming out Sam and I exited the building and stood by the doors waiting for the casket to be loaded. Slowly, the casket, with four pall-bearers on either side came into view and passed through the front doors.

I took one last look at the crowd assembling around the hearse when my eye caught a vehicle moving down the street toward the funeral home. What caught my eye was not the vehicle itself, a dirty Ford sedan, but the pace at which it was moving. The street was a four-lane major thoroughfare with a posted speed limit of 40MPH. The car was moving at about 15MPh and traffic was going around it. At first I thought maybe it was someone wanting to get a last look at the casket. I was wrong. As the car approached, an arm extended from the rear window with a gun in it. Before I could react a voice shouted from the vehicle, "TAKE THIS YOU PUNK," and began firing the pistol in the direction of the casket. The pall-bearers dropped the casket and ducked behind it for cover. The mourners, no strangers to gunfire (this isn't their first rodeo) knew to look for cover also, mostly ducking behind the hearse. The closest object I could find was the Roman column and hit the pavement behind it. As several more shots were fired, I worried where Sam was and whether he was safe, but peeping my head out behind the pillar was not an option. I grabbed my radio and blurted into the mike, "Beat 3322 EMERGENCY! SHOTS FIRED . . . OFFICER UNDER FIRE."

All radio transmission stopped. The dispatcher instructed all officers "STAY OFF THE RADIO . . . WE HAVE AN EMERGENCY . . . BEAT 3322 . . . WHAT IS YOUR LOCATION?"

But the rapid gunfire continued. As I tried talking over the radio I knew my voice was being drowned out by the gunfire. For the moment, I felt helpless. (Now, this is the point in all the movies where the officer does a complete summersault in mid-air while returning gunfire and landing gracefully on his feet. But this isn't the movies and I'm not Clint Eastwood). My only concern was for the safety of me and my partner, wherever he was.

Fortunately, our Sergeant was monitoring the radio. "Dispatch, beat 3322 is at a funeral detail, 137th Street and Packer Ave. Send all available units."

At least I knew the cavalry was coming. But as suddenly as it started, the gunfire stopped. After about 20 shots, I heard the squealing of tires as the sedan sped off. I glanced from behind the pillar to see the casket lying on its side with the pall-bearers behind it. The congregation of mourners were stacked on top of each other behind the hearse. I Looked around but didn't see Sam.

"Sam," where you at," I shouted.

The door of the funeral home eased open and Sam stuck his head out. "I'm fine," he reassured me.

I got back on the radio. "Dispatch, we're all right, be on the look-out for a dirty red Ford heading south on Packer Ave."

By now several squad cars were arriving on the scene, lights flashing and sirens blasting. The entire street filled up with squad cars overwhelming the street and blocking traffic in both directions. Several officers streamed from their cars and filled the street securing the perimeter. It warmed my heart to see so many of my fellow officers coming to assist Sam and me. You can criticize the police for many things, but there is one thing we do very well—we take care of each other.

Pushing his way through the sea of officers, our Sergeant walked up to Sam and me. "Are you guys hurt?"

"No, Sarge, me and my partner are fine," I replied

"Good. Now what the hell happened?"

I ran down the events that occurred while the Sergeant listened with a dumbfounded expression on his face. He kept staring at the casket lying on the ground riddled with bullet holes.

The Sergeant addressed Sam, "did you get a good look at the shooter or a license plate number on the car?"

All Sam could say was "I ducked inside the funeral home. I really didn't see much."

Looking at me, the Sergeant asked, "you were outside, did you get a good look at the shooter or car?"

"No Sarge," I answered, "but I did get a good look at that pillar I was hiding behind."

The Sergeant walked away shaking his head.

Sam walked up to the casket to inspect it. After a few moments he looked in my direction and stated, "I count 17 bullet holes."

The only thing good to come out of this was nobody got shot. Well, nobody who was breathing at the time got shot. It seemed the shooter was aiming at the casket and not anyone at the funeral. The point being, whoever messes with us (rival gang) is going to get the same thing.

Sam circled the casket a few times and finally asked me, "how do we write this up? I mean the only person shot was the deceased, and he was dead already. I don't think he will be complaining."

I had to admit it. I was scratching my head about that too. Is it illegal to shoot someone who was already dead? And if you catch the shooter (a big 'if') who would sign the complaint and what would be the charge (kind of like one of those zen riddles)? Sam and I decided to leave that one for the detectives who would be responsible for the investigation to figure out. But there was one thing we did know. The casket, and body inside, contained bullets that would have to be recovered. All bullets must be preserved for ballistics. Ballistics is the process where marks are etched onto the bullet as it leaves the barrel of the gun. Since no two gun barrels are alike (just like fingerprints) each bullet fired leaves distinct marks on that bullet and can later be traced to the gun that fired it. So the casket and its contents would have to be sent to the morgue. There, a technician can recover the evidence.

Sam and I went back inside. The lobby was empty. The man we saw earlier in the dark suit motioned for us to come over. "I'm the director of this establishment," he announced, "can you please come with me officers?"

He led us to a door and into a small office at the back of the building. The room was small, about 8 by 8. A large desk consumed half of the room. Sitting at the desk was the young lady with the black pants suit. She was wearing black lipstick that extended beyond the upper and lower lip line (that's what looked so odd before). Considering what had occurred, she seemed quite composed. In fact, the funeral director seemed more distraught. He was probably thinking a shooting at the funeral home can't be good for business.

The funeral director introduced himself: "I'm Mr. Phillips, the lady is Miss Jenkins, she is the grieving girlfriend . . . the deceased had no other family"

I directed my comments at Miss Jenkins. "I'm sorry for what happened. You can be guaranteed that we will do everything in our power to find the people responsible for this" (of course, I thought to myself, our powers are pretty limited when nobody ever cooperates with the police).

Appearing inconvenienced by the events, she asked "what happens now?"

I looked in Sam's direction for guidance as to how to break the bad news to her, but Sam seemed at a loss for words also. "Well," I started, "unfortunately, the casket and your deceased boyfriend are now part of a crime scene. Which means the casket and remains will have to return to the Medical Examiner's Office. I'm afraid you won't be able to bury your boyfriend today."

I paused, waiting for some reaction, but got none. I continued, "you will have to contact the Medical Examiner's Office tomorrow and they will tell you when the remains will be released."

Seeming a little confused, she asked, "so when the body is released I will have to start all over again, with a wake and burial?"

"Yes," I answered.

"But what if those people come back again and try shooting at the casket again?"

"Well," I suggested, "have you ever considered cremation?"

13

# CHAPTER 3

# The Lost badge

Sam and I were sitting on a couple of bar stools after a busy day of work contemplating the origins of the universe. The place was right across the street from the station house and the customers were all police officers (hopefully off-duty officers). It was a dark and dingy place, but no one came here for the atmosphere. It was simply a place to go after work and unwind. And, most importantly, it was open 24 hours which came in handy with the unusual hours police work (the liquor license issued by the city prohibits being open 24 hours, but the owner was a retired copper, and the patrons were all police, so who was going to complain).

Two officers from our watch entered the place. Sam motioned for Ted and Frank to come join us.

Ted looked down in the dumps.

"Bad day," I commented.

Frank responded, "not one of our better days, but especially bad for my partner, Ted."

"Sit down and tell me all about," as I raised my arm for the bartender to bring over more beers.

Ted went on to explain that he lost his badge today. When the tour of duty was over, Ted went into the locker room, took off his shirt and noticed the badge was gone. He tried to remember where he lost it, but it was a busy day and Ted and his partner handled about 40 calls for service. And you can bet no one in this neighborhood is going to turn it in if they find it. What made matters worse is that Ted lost his badge about eight months ago. He reported it to the Sergeant and received a written reprimand. Losing a second badge meant suspension time, and Ted had a wife and three kinds.

At this point the smart thing to do was for Ted to notify his Sergeant and take the suspension time. But as the night lingered on, and all of us were on our sixth beer, doing the smart thing was off the table. That's when the plan was hatched. Now all the bells and warning alarms should have gone off when a plan is hatched by several drunken cops, but it seemed brilliant at the time.

Tomorrow, operation 'save Ted' would be put in action.

Sam and I attended roll call the next day with the watch, except for Ted who called in saying he would be late—car trouble. This way the Sergeant would not notice Ted did not have a badge on his shirt.

It was a blistery day, about zero degrees out with snow predicted. The cold weather made for a slow day, which fit perfectly into our plans. It was if all the stars had aligned.

Frank and Ted worked the adjacent beat from us, beat 3323. We met up with them right after the sun went down. By now the snow began to fall and the streets were empty. The plan was as follows: At 10:00 P.M. Frank and Ted would call in a foot chase claiming someone threw a rock at the squad car and the offender was fleeing, with Ted and Frank in pursuit. Sam and I would jump on the radio saying we were going to assist. Why the deception? If an officer loses a badge in the performance of his duties, no disciplinary action is taken, and losing a badge while chasing a fleeing offender certainly qualifies for 'in the line of duty.' The fictitious chase would be the perfect cover. Everyone listening to the radio, including the Sergeant, would hear the chase and no one would question how the badge was lost.

Just like clockwork, at exactly 10:00 P.M., Ted got on the radio and stated, "beat 3323 emergency."

The dispatcher cleared all radio traffic, "go ahead with your emergency beat 3323."

"Dispatch, our car was hit with a rock. The offender is a male with a long beard, he's wearing a green coat and black pants, he's heading southbound through a gangway at 130th and Thomas, my partner is in foot pursuit."

"10-4," the dispatcher acknowledged," are there any units in the vicinity to assist beat 3323?"

That was our cue. Sam got on the radio. "Beat 3322, we're close dispatch, we'll assist." But Sam and I were already with Ted and Frank. We were sitting on the corner of 130th and Thomas as the farce continued. Ted got on the radio a few more times, saying the offender was going this way then that way before telling the dispatcher he lost him. As a final act to clinch the deal, Ted got out of the squad car, turned his back toward the passenger door, and kicked the door with his boot like a bucking mule. "That should do it," Ted announced as he eyed the big dent he put in the door.

Sam and I began patting ourselves on the back for the good deed we done when we noticed a car coasting in our direction. It was another squad car. It was the Sergeant.

Perfect, I thought, Ted could run down what happened (more precisely, what we wanted to make the Sergeant believed happened) and Ted would avoid any disciplinary action. As I looked closer, however, I noticed there was somebody in the back seat of the Sergeant's squad car. I turned toward Sam, "who would be riding in the back seat of the Sergeant's squad in the middle of a snowstorm?"

Sam looked as confused as me.

The Sergeant drove his vehicle parallel to Ted and Frank, rolled down the window and said "I got your offender."

I gazed over at Sam; Sam gazed over at Ted; Ted gazed over at Frank. We all gazed the Sergeant. We were speechless.

Sure enough, the Sergeant opened the back door of his squad car and escorted the guy over to Ted's car. "Here you go," he said, "lock him up."

I couldn't believe my eyes. The guy had a long, stringy beard. He was wearing a green rumpled coat and baggy black pants, just like the description Ted gave over the radio.

Ted swallowed hard and asked, "where did you find him, Sarge?"

"He was hiding in a gangway about three blocks away. He smells like he's been drinking. I'm just glad I was nearby. He's all yours."

I didn't know what Ted was going to say, but I hoped it was going to be something brilliant. All he could muster was, "Thanks Sarge."

The Sergeant drove away grinning ear to ear, thinking he just solved a big crime.

17

Ted looked at me for answers. "What do I do with this guy now?"

I recognized the guy the Sergeant caught. He was the area wino. He wasn't curled up in some gangway hiding from the police. He was homeless and looking for a place to keep warm. But putting him in the lock-up overnight might be the best thing for him. A warm bed and a free bologna sandwich (standard fare for all arrestees) would do him some good. In fact, years ago the police used to take homeless drunks and lock them up for the night. The drunks appreciated it. Until the American Civil Liberties Union (ACLU) filed a lawsuit saying that violated their rights. So, instead of locking them up, the drunks went to the hospital. Then the hospitals started to complain. They didn't want some drunk with no medical issues taking up a bed. So no we just live them on the street.

I told Ted, "take him to the lock-up and let him sleep it off. Tomorrow he won't remember any of this anyway." He gets a nice nap for tonight and you don't have to tell the Sergeant we made the whole story up. It's a win-win."

Ted and Frank agreed and carted the drunk off for the night. Once in the station house, they informed the Sergeant how the badge was lost in the chase. The Sergeant wrote the report that the badge was lost 'in the performance of his duties' and Ted was happy.

I was off work the next two days, but the first day back I sat next to Ted at roll-call. He was wearing a shiny new badge. "So, how did things turn out," I inquired to Ted.

"Very well," Ted answered, "although I did feel bad about arresting the wino. But, I figured, I would go to court the next day and inform the judge I wasn't completely sure he was the one who threw the rock. Without my testimony the judge would dismiss the case."

"Did the judge dismiss it?" I asked.

"Not exactly, Ted replied, "I didn't get a chance to testify, the wino pleaded guilty."

# CHAPTER 4

# The Domestic

I was in the process of reading the riot act to some lady for going through a red light and almost hitting our squad car when Sam yelled at me from the car, "let's go, we got a call." I had already made up my mind not to write her a ticket anyway, she looked traumatized from being stopped by the police, and a ticket probably would have put her in a coma. So I handed her the driver's license back and said "go to church and say three Hail Mary's as punishment for your sins." I high-tailed it back to the squad car and asked Sam, "what's up?"

"We got a call of a domestic disturbance, supposedly he's tearing up the house."

Of all the calls we receive, I hated domestics the most. I'd rather go to a call of someone with a gun or and armed robbery in progress. At least with those calls you knew what you were walking into, and back-up cars always assisted. But with domestics, only one car is assigned and you never know what might be waiting for you.

As we approached the address, a two-story structure located on the corner, Sam pointed up to the second floor on the North side of the building A man with two arms extended was holding a portable television set out the window. He was yelling something, but Sam and I were too far away to hear what he was saying. Before we could get any closer, the man dropped the television. It hit the concrete pavement with a loud boom, several pieces broke free and scattered like shrapnel in all directions.

Sam hit the brakes. We were about 100 feet from the building, and any closer would make us a target. The man disappeared inside the residence as Sam and I got out of the car and looked for any other movement in the window. We didn't have to wait long. A window on the East side of the building opened and a small toaster over was launched. It made it to the street and ricochet three times before coming to rest at the curb. I looked at Sam and said, "I checked the weather forecast for today, it didn't say anything about raining appliances."

Sam was not amused. "How the hell are we going to stop this guy?"

"Good point, "I conceded, "let's walk down a couple of houses, through the gangway to the alley, then back up to the rear of the building."

As we maneuvered our way to the back of the building, a young woman in bare foot and a robe was standing there holding a cell phone. She looked in our direction and said "I called the police."

I kept one eye on her and one eye on the second floor window. "What's going on, besides the obvious?"

Before she could speak the back window opened. "Watch out," I shouted. Sam grabbed the woman by the arm and dragged her around the corner of the building. I was close behind. Sam and I peeked around the corner to see a microwave oven hoisted out the window. The oven hit the soft lawn and bounced back toward the building hitting the downspout of the rain gutter. The downspout dislodged from the building and came down like a falling tree toward us. With no time to react, the downspout hit Sam square on top of his head.

"Dam, are you all right partner?"

Fortunately, the gutter was aluminum and Sam gestured he was fine.

The woman went on to explain that she was home, in bed, with another man when her boyfriend came home unexpectedly. That explains why she was only wearing a robe.

"And where's the other man?" Sam asked.

"He ran out the door ahead of me."

"Just out of curiosity," Sam continued, "Where is he at now?"

"For all I know he's still running."

Before formulating a plan of attack, I needed to gather some intel as to what we were up against.

I asked, "What's you boyfriend's name?"

"Roy."

Now for the important questions: "Does Roy have any weapons up there? You know . . . like guns, rifles, explosives, nuclear warheads."

She shook her head, "no, nothing like that."

"How about dogs?"

"We don't have dogs, but the landlord who resides on the first floor does. I think it's a rottweiler. But he usually keeps him in a cage."

"Are you hurt?"

"No. I'm fine. I grabbed my robe and cell phone and ran out of the house. All those things he's throwing out the window, they're mine. Since I'm not there, he taking it out on my property."

"Gee, you think," I said sarcastically.

Our options were limited. Sam and I were going to have to get in there and arrest him before furniture started exiting the window. I tried the back door; it was locked. I knew what the answer was, but I had to ask. "You wouldn't happen to have the key to the door?"

Standing there only in bathrobe, the woman just glared at me.

Sam and I quickly surveyed the door. It was a six-panel oak door. Not very strong, considering it was an outside door. The door knob lock looked pretty weak as well, and, to our benefit, there was no dead bolt. Sam positioned himself behind me as braced to kick the door in. Grabbing both sides of the frame, I lifted my foot and drove my foot as hard as I could near the lock. My foot missed the lock and hit one of the panels. The door didn't budge, but my foot went through the panel and my thigh lodged in the door. My first instinct was to pull my leg out but I felt a sudden pain in my thigh. The wood seemed to coalesce around my leg and pulling back forced splinters into my leg. My leg was stuck. I was pretty much in panic mode now, and it was about to get worse. I heard the barking of a dog and the sound was getting louder. The barking sound wasn't some high-pitched tone of some lap dog. It was a deep baritone bark of a big dog. And the fact that the sound was getting louder made me realize the dog was getting closer. As I assessed the situation it didn't look good.

My leg was stuck. Check.

There's some guy in there really ticked off. Check.

There's some big dog drawing a bead on my leg. Checkmate.

"Do something," I yelled to Sam.

As I felt a tug on my leg I realized the dog had his jaws on my pants leg. Sam backed up several feet and took a run at the door. He lowered his right shoulder and hit the door square, right above my leg. The door caved in pulling me forward. I landed on top of the door and Sam landed on top of me. While Sam solved one problem—we were now inside—the other problem still existed. My leg was under the door with the dog.

"The dog Sam, get the dog," I screamed.

Sam lifted the door with me on top and drew his weapon. All I heard was POP.POP.POP. Sam fired three times. The dog let out a large squeal and emerged from the under the door. He staggered a few feet and disappeared under the stairway. A trail of blood stained the floor.

"I hope that's the dog's blood and not mine," I told Sam.

"I couldn't miss from that range," Sam replied.

Sam helped me up and pulled several of the wood splinters from around the door. I was able to free myself. In all the commotion I almost forget why we were here. There's still a guy up there we have to arrest. With my legging throbbing, Sam and I made our way up the staircase to the second floor apartment. I tried the door handle, it was locked.

"Oh no," I informed Sam, I'm not doing that again."

Sam pounded on the door with his fist. "Open up, it's the police.

No response. The apartment was dead silent.

Sam directed me out of the way and hit the door with his shoulder. The wood around the doorknob gave way and the door swung open.

"Show-off," I whispered as I scanned the apartment from the doorway. The first room was the kitchen and there was no sign of life. The room was a mess. The kitchen table was overturned, the refrigerator was knocked on its side, and kitchen utensils were strewn all over the floor. I un-holstered my weapon and entered. Ahead was a narrow hallway with a door on either side. The drywall on both sides had holes the size of a fist in them. Sam and I proceeded slowly. I motioned for Sam to check the door on the right while I watched his back. He entered the bathroom and checked behind the shower curtain—no one. I entered the door on the left while Sam stood guard. I looked in the closet and under the bed—no one. We moved cautiously toward the front of the house. Sam and I entered the living room. At the front of the room, a man was sitting in a lounge chair with his feet up.

Sam raised his weapon, "don't move, let me see your hands."

The man was not as I pictured him. He was rather diminutive, maybe five-and-a-half feet tall and skinny. The man raised his hands above his head and Sam moved closer. While Sam kept his weapon trained on the man, I approached from the side.

"Get up slowly," Sam ordered.

The man rose to his feet. I circled around and approached him from the side. As I got close, I reached out and grabbed his wrist with a twisting motion causing the man to flinch and bend forward. I put my other hand in his back and forced him, face down, onto the floor. He laid there limp on the floor as I put the handcuffs on. Standing him up, the man looked content as his eyes swept across the room admiring his destructive ability. The man offered no resistance. Either he was too tired from breaking everything, or gave up because there was nothing left to break.

Back down the steps and out the back door, I led the man into the backyard. The woman ran toward my partner and I and threw her arms around the man. She asked, "are you O.K. Roy, the police didn't hurt you did they?"

"Excuse me, "I interrupted, "but he's the only one who isn't hurt!"

I could tell my protesting was going to fall on deaf ears. I have seen that look before—the look of love and forgiveness in her face. Now that Sam and I did the dirty work of getting in the apartment and stopping his tantrum, the lady was happy and did not want to see him go to jail. Sam and I have seen this movie a million times. But I had ask, "listen lady, do you want so sign a complaint against your boyfriend here?"

A curt "no" was the response."

Sam looked at me with disbelief. There was no way I was going to let this guy go. My leg is still bleeding, which means a trip to the emergency room is in order. Two doors are broken in, and sometime in the near future the landlord is going to come home and 'man's best friend' is not going to be greeting him at the door. Unfortunately, our State is not a mandatory arrest State. That is, the police do not sign complaints for the victim. In other States, if any assault takes place at a domestic and the victim refuses to sign the complaint, the officer is required by law to sign the complaint and arrest the spouse. The assumption being, the victim may not sign out of fear of retaliation. Even if this were a mandatory arrest State, there's no evidence the victim was assaulted. The only crime was damaging the house, and for that you need a signed complaint.

The man turned his back toward me waiting to be released. But instead of taking the handcuffs off I addressed Sam. "Go get the squad car partner, he's going to jail"

The man protested, "you heard my old lady, she won't sign a complaint. What are you arresting me for?"

Thinking of the appliances scattered throughout the street and sidewalk, I responded with a one word answer, "Littering."

# CHAPTER 5

## A person shot

It was 7:00 P.M. Dusk started to settle over our beat, and the vultures of the night started to come out. Radio traffic increased as the dispatcher starting talking fast. Then, it was our turn. "Beat 3322."

Sam answered, "be gentle with us dispatch" (make it an easy assignment).

"Handle the call of shots fired, 12214 S. Cedar."

I glared over at Sam, "you had to jinx us, didn't you."

While Sam smirked, I hit the emergency lights and siren and headed for the call. The block the call originated from is a series of row-houses up and down both sides of the streets—and a notorious drug block. It was a never closed supermarket of marijuana laced with PCP (a powerful controlled substance that intensified the high). Recently, the local newspaper did a big expose on drug trafficking in the city. The corner of 122 Street and Cedar was high on the list. For the story, the newspaper reporter interviewed one of the drug dealers (where the drug dealer sits behind a curtain and they alter his voice so he couldn't be identified). The dealer proudly proclaimed his involvement. In his words, he was doing the public a favor—giving them what they wanted. Of course the article went on to rip the police for not shutting down the illegal drugs. But it's not a matter of allowing the crime to continue, it's a matter of catching them. The area has several look-outs on every corner that whistle whenever the police come near. Their early warning system is better than the missile defense system at NORAD. Plus, the dealers never carry the product (drugs) on them. And the person who delivers the drugs never touches the money. When a buyer pulls up, the moneyman collects the cash and yells to another down the block. The second person goes to one of multiple locations down the block and brings the product to the buyer. This way, the seller never has more than a small amount of narcotics on him at one time. The dealer knows if he gets caught with the drugs before the transaction is complete, the amount he is carrying is very small, which is a less serious charge (possession of drugs) then getting caught with a large amount (delivery of drugs). And, more importantly to the dealer, since the person bringing the drugs to the car never touched the money, the cash cannot be confiscated as drug profits. Who said criminals are stupid? And to make matters worse, after the newspaper article was published, the amount of activity on the block has increased immensely—nothing like free publicity. The drug trafficking is so efficient the dealers on the block own a pick-up truck with a snowplow on front. During the winter months, the dealers plow the public street around the area so customers can drive safely to the site.

While still en route, the dispatcher called again. "Be aware beat 3322, we are getting multiple calls of shots fired from the block."

That was a bad sign. It is not uncommon to receive a bogus call of shots fired. One call could be someone playing with the police, or sometimes, criminals themselves make fake calls to divert police away from some other area while they commit crimes. But multiple calls meant it was the real deal. As I got within a few blocks of the address, I shut off the emergency lights and siren. If someone was there with a gun, I didn't want to become a target with our emergency lights flashing.

I turned onto the block and the streets were empty. No noises, no one outside walking, no cars moving. It looked like a ghost town. I expected a tumble weed to go rolling by at any second.

Sam stated, "It looks like a black hole in space."

As the squad car crept down the block, I could see all the blinds and shades drawn on the row houses. This is a neighborhood where people set their watches by random gunfire. Something bad happened or was about to happen to drive them all inside. Halfway down the block, Sam pointed ahead and bellowed, "over there, two guys fighting."

I looked further down the block where Sam was pointing and witnessed the silhouettes of two bodies in the darkness. They were struggling with each other. As I drove toward the struggle, the light of a muzzle flash was seen between the two bodies followed by the report of the gun. One of the bodies fell to the ground and the second silhouette ran down the block and around the corner.

Sam bailed out of the car after the fleeing offender. I got on the radio and asked for assistance, "beat 3322, shots fired, I got a man down, I need an ambulance, my partner is in foot pursuit." I went to assist the man lying on the ground, "where you shot", I barked. Standing over the man, I realized I made a mistake that could have cost me my life: I assumed. The man on the ground in front of me had a gun in his hand. He wasn't the victim, he was the shooter, apparently tripping and falling after firing the gun. He lifted the gun in my direction and heaved the gun upward over the roofline of the row house. Completely caught off guard and luckily not tending any bullet wounds, I froze for a moment. The sound of sirens approaching brought me back to reality. I quickly jumped on top of him and put handcuffs on both wrists. Getting back on the radio, "Dispatch, let responding units know I have the offender and my partner is chasing the victim."

Thinking I made a mistake, the dispatcher replied, "you want to repeat that."

"You heard my squad, I have the offender, my partner is after the victim. I'm going to need a fire truck here also."

Several squad cars arrived to assist, but the worst was over. After putting the offender in my squad car one of the assisting officers called me back over to the scene. "Somebody was definitely shot," pointing to a small pool of fresh blood on the ground. Another officer added, "there's a trail of blood leading down the block."

By now Sam had returned to meet me. He was out of breath. "I lost him after a couple of blocks," he said.

"Some guy who was shot outran you?" I asked incredulously.

"What do you mean shot," Sam responded.

I pointed to the blood on the ground. "The man in our car is the offender, he had the gun, the person you were chasing is the victim who was shot."

"Go figure," was all Sam could say.

Sam and I followed the trail of blood for a couple of blocks where it stopped in a courtyard shared by several houses. "Either he's a fast healer or he's holed up in one of these houses," I grumbled. But not knowing which one left us at a dead end. It was probably for the best. If we could pinpoint the house, we would need a search warrant to make entry. Asking a judge to come back to court at night to sign a search warrant would not make him happy. And explaining to him we needed the warrant to find a victim who was shot, he would send us for a breathalyzer test. Sam and I gave up the search and headed back to the scene. Walking back, the ambulance I requested pulled up. The paramedic asked, "where's the guy shot?"

"Don't be a smart ass," Sam answered.

A few minutes later the fire truck arrived. "Where's the fire?" the firefighter laughed.

Fire humor I guess. "No fire," I said, "but I could use your ladder to find a gun on the roof."

The fireman positioned the extension ladder up against the building and I climbed onto the flat roof. I searched the roof from front to back. No gun. The roof did pitch from the front to the back so I had Sam search the back yard in case the gun slid off. No gun. I studied the chimney on the roof. It was a brick structure that only protruded about a foot above the roof. The long rectangular shape made me believe it vented a fireplace. I climbed down the building and knocked On the door.

An eldery man opened the door a crack stretching a chain that was still attached. At last I caught I break, I thought to myself. The older gentleman was not the usual criminal element around here and chances of him cooperating were good.

"What you want?" he asked in a frail voice.

"This may seem like a strange question, but can I look up your chimney?"

He slammed the door in my face.

Foiled again. Sam and I thanked the other officers for their help and we wondered what to do next. We had no victim and no gun. I leaned into the squad car at the man in the back seat, "what were you two fighting about?"

His reply: "I don't know nothin' about nothin."

I thought about correcting him; after all, that attempt at a sentence was a double negative which means he does know something, but why waste oxygen. Sam and I knew the person shot would eventually turn up at the hospital to get that bullet removed, but we had no charges to hold this guy right now. There's only one trauma center on this side of town, and most victims who show up at the hospital have no insurance and refuse to give their name. The trauma victims know the hospital has to treat them anyway. It has gotten so bad that the hospital goes through several letters of the alphabet when assigning names to patients who refuse to identify themselves. Every day, the hospital starts with Adam Doe, then Bob Doe, then Charlie Doe (and yes, when they get to "j" they use John Doe). So when the person shot here tonight finally winds up at the hospital he will be just another victim in the crowd.

I opened the back door of the squad car, removed the handcuffs from the guy and pointed for him to leave. While he strolled down the street I shouted, "have a nice day."

# CHAPTER 6

# Traffic tickets

About one day a month Sam and I get assigned the traffic car as a reminder that part of our job is to write tickets. Contrary to public belief, police officers do not have a quota for writing tickets. But ticket writing is encouraged by the Sergeant since it brings in revenue for the city. Having debunked that myth, I have to admit, the purpose of the traffic car is twofold: One, to respond to traffic accidents and do reports; and two, to write traffic tickets. The upside of working the traffic car for the day is no radio assignments. So Sam and I grabbed our ticket books and were getting ready for a fun-filled day of traffic stops.

Generally, most of the cars Sam and I stop for traffic violations get a warning. As most officers will tell you, it's not the violation that dictates who gets a ticket, but it comes down to the attitude of the driver. If some poor schmuck is on his way to or from work and is respectful, I would not issue a ticket. Conversely, when I pull someone over and the first words out their mouths is "why you hassling me," or "don't you have something better to do," or my personal favorite, "the only reason you stopped be is because I'm black, or brown, or green, or whatever," they are going to get rung up (ticketed).

Leaving the station, the desk Sergeant handed us a piece of paper with an address on it, "some lady called the station, she was involved in a traffic accident."

"We'll take care of it Sarge," Sam replied.

Sam and I headed to the scene of the traffic accident. On the way, a black Cadillac blew by us on the inner lane like we were standing still. Before I could say a word, Sam hit the emergency lights and sped up to catch the car. Sam shook his head. "We don't have to look for traffic violators, they'll find us." The car pulled to the curb and Sam positioned the squad car behind. Sam got out and approached the driver while I took a position at the rear passenger side. Watching through the rear window, I could see the driver was alone. He was fiddling with something on the passenger seat and then began fidgeting his hands back and forth in a waving motion. I cautioned Sam, "be careful partner, he's up to something." But before Sam could reach the driver, the driver's door swung open and the driver literally fell out of the car onto the pavement. I put my hand on the butt of my gun getting ready to draw when the driver got up from the ground and slammed the door shut.

"What the hell is going on," Sam blared.

"Officer, I apologize, but there's a bee in my car. I didn't want to get stung."

Just when I thought I heard it all, a traffic violator comes up with a new excuse.

Sam looking dubious also, remarked, "at least that's original."

"No really," the man pleaded, see for yourself."

I peeked into the car and sure enough a bee was buzzing around in there. I opened the passenger door and backed off. The bee flew out the door and on its way. Unfortunately for the driver, while opening the door, I spotted what he was doing when we approached the vehicle. I reached in and removed a plastic bottle. The bottle itself looked innocent enough, about the size of a prescription bottle, but the cap had several holes in it. I held up the bottle so Sam and the driver could see it. "You let the bee out of the bottle didn't you?"

The man turned blue. "I don't "know what you mean?"

"Sure you do, the holes in the bottle are air holes for the bee. You keep a bee in the car and let it out anytime the police stop you. I bet this isn't the first time you used this trick."

"It was just a joke officer, I can't afford to pay a ticket."

Sam and I walked back to the squad car out of earshot of the driver. "what you think," I asked Sam.

"I got to give him an 'A' for originality," Sam admitted, "I say let him go. Besides we got an accident to waiting for us."

I gave the driver back his bottle and added, "go find another bee."

Sam and I reached the site of the traffic crash. It was a one-car accident. The driver ran her vehicle up the curb and side swiped a tree. The female driver, about 20-something and attractive, was nicely dressed in a blue blouse with matching high heels. She was a little shaken up from the accident but was uninjured. Eying the tire tracks in the grass, I could tell the compact car narrowly missed hitting the huge oak tree head on. As usual, the driver claims she was driving down the street obeying every traffic law that existed, and a few yet to be enacted, when a car cut her off forcing her to swerve and strike the tree.

"Sam asked the woman," can you describe the car that cut you off."

"Not really, it was a big car, I think dark in color."

With a description like that the other driver should be in custody shortly. Sam and I refer to these types of accidents as "phantom crashes." Whenever a driver is involved in a one-car accident, they always claim some mysterious car caused it. Nobody will ever admit they were on a cell phone, or changing the dial on the radio, or sight-seeing out the window and were distracted, that would be too embarrassing. So, instead, the driver comes up with the fictitious car that did it. The description of the car is always vague and never includes a license plate number that could be traced. Of course there's no way to dispute the driver's story so Sam and I always write the cause of accident on the report "phantom vehicle."

I was doing the traffic report while Sam was sweet talking the young woman trying to get a phone number. I interrupted Sam. "Can I talk to you back at the car, partner?"

Back at the car, I teased Sam, "she's not your type,"

What makes you say that?"

"For one thing, she's already lying to you."

"You mean the phantom car thing?" Sam assumed, "it's possible she was cut off."

Sam was so smitten he missed the obvious. And the fact I believed she was lying didn't make her a bad person. "Go back and talk to her," I instructed Sam, "and take a close look at her face and the contents of the front seat."

Sam headed back and made some small talk with the lady, including asking for her phone number. The two really seemed to be hitting it off. I finished the report as Sam returned. "What did you see," I asked."

Sam looked a little deflated. "Her lipstick was smeared".

"Very good . . . and?"

"There was an open tube of lipstick on the front seat."

Playing Sherlock Holmes I asked "and based upon this evidence what do you deduce?"

Getting annoyed, Sam replied, "you know what it means."

"Yes, but I want to admit it."

Finally Sam burst, "she was putting lipstick on in the rear view mirror when she hit the tree . . . there was no car that cut her off. You happy?"

It wasn't a matter of being happy. I just wanted Sam to know the truth. Hey, maybe they will start dating, fall in love and have a great story to tell their kids of how they met.

Sam started the car and pulled away. Passing the young lady, she screamed something at us and Sam snapped his head backwards to see what was going on. The squad car veered to the left hitting the curb. "Watch Out," I yelled as the tire made impact with the curb and ripped the steering wheel out of Sam's hand. The wheels cut hard to the left. Sam slammed the brakes to the floor but by then the car was off the street and onto a parkway covered with grass. The wheels locked and the car continued skidding forward. "This was going be close" I shouted as a utility pole was several feet ahead and closing fast. The pole hit the driver's-side front fender at the corner and buckled the front end and hood. The airbags deployed with a large whoosh sound and the car finally came to rest with the pole embedded in the front fender.

"You all right?" Sam asked.

"Been better, but nothing is broken."

The entire frame of the squad car crumpled a few inches, forcing the side panels of the car into the door panels. Neither door would open. Sam and I climbed out the windows of the squad car to assess the damage. The car looked totaled. Green liquid was spraying from the radiator and some brown fluid was forming a puddle under the engine. I felt like I should take my gun out and shoot it to put it out of its misery.

The young lady who was shouting ran up and asked if we were fine. We assured her we were fine. I had to ask, "what were you shouting?"

Holding the piece of paper up and eying Sam, "It's my phone number, you forgot to take it." Sam accepted the piece of paper from the lady and put it in his shirt pocket.

"Well, now that your love life is on track," I announced, "what the hell do we going to tell the Sergeant?"

Sam glanced at me, then the lady. He turned his attention back to me and said, "we were cut off by the phantom vehicle."

# CHAPTER 7

# The drug house

I knocked on the door of the tactical office located in the basement of the station house. One of the officers opened the door for Sam and me to enter. Eight tactical officers and a Sergeant were huddled around a desk in full riot gear. The gear consisted of a black wrap around bulletproof vest that puffed out at the chest (they resembled the ninja turtle outfits worn by the cartoon characters). To go along with the vests were special gun belts that strapped to the thighs to carry larger weapons with long clips (the clip held 50 rounds of ammo) and hand held bullet proof shields.

"Expecting trouble," Sam quipped.

The tactical Sergeant, a no-nonsense ex-marine with a crew cut shot back, "you know why you are here, sit down."

We knew exactly why we were here, to serve as entry officers for a search warrant that was about to be executed. In the past, tactical officers would make forced entry into a house without the assistance of beat officers. However, on several occasions, the occupants of the building would fight with the tactical officers, or even shoot at them. After being arrested, the offenders would come to court and tell the judge they didn't know the men in the funny black vests were the police, they thought they were being robbed (it is common for robbers to target drug houses—that's where the money is). To prevent this, the department mandated that two uniformed officers would be assigned to a tactical team when a warrant was served. The two uniformed officers would make entry first and there would be no doubt it was the police. So if Sam or I get shot, stabbed, bitten, or the victim of any blunt trauma, we should be comforted by the thought our attackers could not plea self-defense. For some reason, I was not eased by that reasoning.

The Sergeant began the briefing. "The house we are going to hit is a drug house. We did several controlled buys at the house over the past month with marked money."

A controlled buy is where an undercover officer purchases narcotics with money where the serial numbers have been recorded. It takes a lot of guts to be an undercover officer. The officer must assume he will be searched before the deal goes down, so he cannot have a weapon or police radio on him, which means if things go south he is on his own. Going alone into a drug house with no way of communicating with other officers is very risky, but necessary, to close down the drug house. The buys are needed to establish probable cause to obtain the warrant. And marked money is used to trace the cash. Dope dealers, who deal in large amounts of money, can't go to a bank and deposit it. Well, they could, but any cash transaction over 10,000 dollars requires filling out a form that is forwarded to the federal government. Hence, the money has to be laundered, which usually entails buying phony, and in some cases, legitimate businesses to funnel the money through. That way, it all appears legitimate.

The Sergeant pointed at a bulletin board at the front of the room. Multiple pictures of the house were taped there showing a view from all sides. It was a one story bungalow with burglar bars on the doors and windows.

The Sergeant continued. "The officer who made the undercover buys in the house tells us there are three men inside. They are heavily armed with handguns and rifles, and there are at least two vicious pit bulls in the house." The Sergeant passed around a dossier of the investigation. The file contained pictures of the three men and their criminal records. The three men have extensive criminal records, including attempt murder, armed robbery and delivery of a controlled substance. Included were pictures and license plate numbers of the vehicles they drove (dope dealers always lease cars. If you caught delivering narcotics the car is impounded and can be confiscated. By leasing, and not owning, they don't care if the police take the car—it's not theirs).

Sam looked over at me, "is it too late to go home sick."

"I hear you partner," I answered. Looking at the pictures on the bulletin board, "how the hell are we going to get in that fortress without an airstrike?"

"Everyone grab a battering ram on the way out, the Sergeant instructed.

"You had to ask," Sam remarked as we headed for the door.

The staging area for the operation was a lot a couple of doors down and across the street from the drug house. Several overgrown bushes ran along the front giving good cover. From this vantage point, we could see the house clearly through the brush. As I peeked through the bush, I could see the front windows had blinds that were shuttered. Instead of pulling up in front of the drug house and bailing out of the cars, the plan, according to the sergeant, was to nonchalantly walk across the street and hit the door with the battering ram—a good plan for the tactical team, not so much for Sam and I who would make initial entry.

Crouched behind the bushes with several mosquitos circling, the Sergeant asked, "does anyone have any last questions?"

I shot my hand up like a giddy school kid.

"What's your question?"

"Far be it for me to tell you how to do your job . . ."

The Sergeant interrupted, "VERY FAR BE IT."

I continued, "instead of going to the mountain, why don't we have the mountain come to us."

A look of agitation crossed the sergeant's face, "care to explain that?"

Knowing the mindset of the dope dealer (Sam and I have been doing this for many years) as soon as we hit that door we are going to be attacked by the occupants and the dogs are going to be let loose. Meanwhile, someone in the house is going to be flushing the drugs down the toilet. So I had a plan. "Listen, sarge," I pleaded, "why don't we get the water department out here to shut off the water to the house. Then we call the occupants of the dope house and say the police are coming."

The Sergeant looked intrigued. Sam looked skeptical. The tactical team was swatting mosquitos.

I had to admit it was a risky plan. Tipping off the dope dealers could backfire, but going through that front door was just as risky.

The sergeant hesitated as he pondered my idea. Finally, he spoke, "call the water department and have them meet you at the end of the block."

I got on my cell phone and called the water department. I might have mentioned something about a water main break and that the block was about to be submerged. I figured it was the only way to get them here fast; it worked. The foreman on the truck was a little mad, but when I explained it was an emergency, albeit not a water emergency, he appeared to understand, to a point. He declared," I'm not going to get shot trying to shut the water off."

"Not to worry," I assured him, "I know there's a shut off main in the front yard, just tell me how to do it."

The foreman retrieved a metal pole from the truck. It was about six feet long with a cross-bar handle on one end and a hook on the other end. The procedure seemed simple enough. The hooked is lowered down to reach the water pipe. On the top of the water pipe is a metal ring attached to a valve. Like threading a needle, the hook passes through the ring and the pole is turned clockwise until resistance is met.

"Got it," I replied, "but there's something else I'm going to need."

"No that's it," he insisted.

"What I need is your hat and coat. I can't walk up to the house in a police uniform."

Reluctantly, the foreman acquiesced. As I pushed the hat as far down as I could to cover my eyes, and zipped the coat up to my collar, I headed for the house with the pole in my hand. Trying to appear smug and uncaring (that's what every government employees looks like) I walked up to the house and located the grate in the front yard. Getting on my knees I removed the grate and stuck the pole in the ground. As I hooked the ring, I suddenly panicked. Did he say clockwise or counter clockwise? I couldn't remember. My heart began to pound. Do something was all I could think. I turned the pole to the left. Nothing, it wouldn't move. I looked up at the house wondering what to do if someone exited, but the door remained shut and the blinds closed. I had to do something fast, so I turned the handle to the right. I could feel the valve turn. I continued twisting the handle until it stopped. I put the grate back on and walked away. I wanted to turn to see if anybody was watching, but that would appear suspicious. I kept my eyes straight and headed for the end of the block. Reaching the foreman, and after a momentary pause for my blood pressure to return to normal, I thanked him and returned to the bushes. Sam and the sergeant were waiting for me.

"Water off," the sergeant inquired.

"Got it, nobody will be flushing a toilet in there."

"We better move fast," the sergeant added, "before someone in there needs to use the bathroom." The sergeant opened the file he brought along. "Here's the cell phone number of one of the dealers in the house.

Sam removed his cell phone from his pocket and dialed the number. Trying to sound like a tough thug, he spoke into the phone, "Five-0 man, Five-0, get out of the house" (Five-0 is slang for police, it originated from the television series Hawaii Five-O about the Honolulu police). While I was playing water department, several of the tactical officers had fanned out. Some were concealed under the porch down the block and some waited in the alley behind the house. Since the drug dealers cars were parked in front, we assumed if they bolted they would come right toward us. A few minutes went by with no activity. Then, suddenly, Sam elbowed me in the side as he pointed to the house. The blinds in front opened then quickly closed.

"This is it," the sergeant warned, "get ready."

He was right. The front door opened. A hand reached out and unlocked the burglar bars on the front door and a man stepped out. I quickly recognized him as one the dealers from the sergeant's file.

The sergeant got on the radio to his officers, "they are coming out, get ready."

Standing in the front yard, the man looked up and down the block. The heavy leather coat he was wearing was out of place on such a hot day. He was concealing something. He walked slowly toward the street and two more men exited the building. One was carrying a large black plastic bag swung over his shoulders. The sergeant screamed into the radio, "NOW. NOW. NOW."

Sam and I burst through the bushes with our guns out. Two more officers appeared from under the porch, one on our left and one on our right, and two came running up the street. From the gangway behind the men, four more officers approached. All of us yelling "POLICE . . . DON'T MOVE."

The men were stunned. Seeing police closing in from all directions they stood motionless. "Get your hands up the sergeant screamed." The man with the bag dropped it and all three raised their hands. The tactical officers pushed all three to the ground and handcuffed them. During a search the man with the leather coat had two .45 caliber semi-automatics in his waistband. The sergeant retrieved the bag and opened it. Tightly wrapped in duct tape were six pouches the size of a football.

"What could this be?" the sergeant asked rhetorically. He pulled a knife from his pocket and cut into one of the pouches. Small granules of white powder spilled out. Pure Cocaine.

The three men were led back to the house and laid face down on the floor in the front room. A methodical search of the house was conducted. The pit bulls were tied up in the basement and didn't even bark while we searched the house. They looked in bad shape, with bites marks on their faces and bodies. Apparently they were used for dog fighting, a big sport among drug dealers. Several more handguns were found in the house.

Toting the weapons, drugs and offenders out of the house, what happened next really surprised me. Several of the neighbors on the block came out of their houses. To our delight, they began applauding us. Sick and tired of the criminals running the neighborhood, they were genuinely happy to see the police.

Sam turned philosophical. "See, why are we always so cynical and think the worst of the people on our beat?" Sam asked me.

Before I could respond, the sergeant yelled from the alley, "call for a car to transport these arrestees to the station."

I yelled back, "why don't we take them in ourselves?"

"Can't. While we were searching the house someone stole the tires off of our cars."

# CHAPTER 8

## The lost child

When most people hear the word 'police' they conjure up ideas of cops and robbers, along with thoughts of chasing down criminals and rescuing damsels in distress. Television shows and movies either glamorize the police with car chases and shoot-outs, or demonize the police with brutality and corruption. But most calls for service are from citizens who need help and don't know where to turn. Today, for Sam and me, was no exception. The dispatcher called, "beat 3322 see the lady regarding a lost child." As I acknowledged the assignment, I thought to myself, I've ripped more pants and shirts in my career bending down under porches and cars looking for lost children then fighting with criminals.

The address of the call was in an area of our beat that Sam and I rarely see. Why? Because there is seldom a crime problem there. Why? (I know I'm getting redundant) because the two block area is like an island. One side is bounded by a shallow retention pond, on the other side by railroad tracks, and a third side by a wooded area. With three sides dead-ends, there is only entrance to the area, almost like an urban gated community. The significance of that is criminals stay away. Having only one avenue of escape is usually detrimental to a criminal's freedom. It's like the roach motel for bag guys, the criminals check in but they don't check out.

Sam and I arrived at the curb of a well-kept home and manicured lawn. A long driveway led to the house which was situated at the back

43

of the lot. We walked up the driveway. Several dolls were lying at the foot of the driveway next to a small tricycle. Further up, a chalk hop-scotch was drawn on the pavement. Reaching the front of the house I could see a young woman peering out the window. Not waiting for us to reach the door, she sprang from the house. Her look was panic-stricken and her voice quivered as she spoke. "My daughter is missing. She was playing on the front lawn and now she's gone."

"Slow down," Sam said, "start from the beginning and tell me what happened?"

"Sarah, my daughter, was playing on the front lawn and I was watching her from the house. The phone rang and I went to answer it. I was only gone a minute and when I returned she was gone. She's only four years old."

Thinking of the obvious I asked, "could she have gone to a neighbor's or friend's house, or could a relative have picked her up?"

"No . . . No . . . I taught her to never go anywhere without me. She would never leave on her own. And her father and I are divorced, and he lives in another city over 100 miles away.

Sam and I escorted her back into the house to get as many details as possible. The little girl was wearing a white shirt with red pants. She was about three feet tall with black hair in a ponytail.

"We need you to stay home in case she returns home or someone calls" Sam instructed the mother. "She couldn't have wondered too far, we will find her."

My partner and I left her at the kitchen table and headed back to the car. Several thoughts crossed my mind, and no of them were good. The three-sided dead end which made the area safe worried me. From the retention pond behind the house, to the trains tracks a block down, to the dense forest area a block up, are all areas that attract young, curious minds.

Sam looked at me and said "we are going to need help, a lot of help."

I got on the radio and asked for additional cars to aid in the search. The dispatcher assigned three additional cars. As we waited for the help, Sam had a worried expression on his face. "You know somebody took her."

"I don't think so. Her mother was gone only a minute and was right inside the house. If someone grabber her, she would have screamed and the mother would have heard that."

"That's why my money is on a relative," Sam responded, the girl didn't scream because she knew the person."

Sam had a good point. When a child disappears, the most likely suspect is the spouse. When an ex-husband or ex-boyfriend takes a child, it usually has less to do with the child and more to do with revenge—a way to get back at the mother. Sam went back inside to get the address of the ex-husband. The information was given to the dispatcher, who would send a point-to-point message (a way of sending a radio message to another police agency via radio transmission). The outside police agency was instructed to see if the ex-husband was home and the missing girl was there.

While we had only a few hours of daylight left and time was critical, I decided to use all the resources available. If there's some 4 year old out there lost, she would be alone and frightened. Pulling out all the stops, I requested the Marine Unit (officers with scuba gear) to check the retention pond behind the house. I also requested the police helicopter to do a fly over, especially in the densely wooded area, with their FLIR (Forward Looking Infra-Red) equipment. The FLIR system picks up heat the body gives off. And lastly, I asked for a canine officer. Maybe a dog could pick up the girl's scent.

Sam, trying to take the department's perspective, said "that's a lot of manpower and equipment you are requesting."

"I know, but what if it was your daughter?"

Sam nodded in agreement.

The assist cars arrived and every officer was given one block area to search. We spread out through the neighborhood and rang every doorbell, checked under every porch and any cubby hole large enough to hold a four year. The only thing I encountered were nests of bugs. I think I was able to identify several new species of insects never seen before under dark porches. While the search continued, the dispatcher called, "beat 3322 meet the marine unit back at the house."

I returned to the house and saw Sam talking to two officers from the marine unit. They were seated in an SUV with a trailer hitched to the back. The trailer was carrying a small watercraft with an outboard motor on the back. Sam briefed the officer and got them up to date. The marine officers found a place to launch the boat in the retention pond behind the house and began a search. Just then, a large roar from the sky was heard. The police helicopter was hovering overhead to begin their search of the wooded area. While no word on the girl yet, I felt confident everything that could be done was being done.

Sam and I returned to the house to see if the mother heard any news. She was still sitting in the kitchen, her eyes were tearing and her hands were trembling. Sam put her arm around her and squeezed. "We started looking, we will find her," he stated with conviction in his voice.

"I know you will," but the worried look on her face conveyed otherwise.

Returning back outside, a news truck had pulled up behind our squad car. The local news stations frequently monitor the police radio and respond to crime scenes. "Great," I told Sam, "all we need is some reporter sticking a microphone in the mother's face."

Sam said, "you have the most seniority partner, it's your responsibility to give a statement."

Department policy does state that if any comments are given to the news media, the most senior officer on the scene is to give the statement. I guess the department figures the most seasoned officer is less likely to say something stupid (obviously Sam and I were not taken into consideration when the policy was established).

"Nice try" I responded, "you have the same seniority as me."

"Yes, but you can bullshit with the best of them."

He had me there. I walked over to the news truck as the reporter was testing her mic while a man was pointing a portable camera in her face. Behind them, a technician was sitting behind a control panel in the rear of the truck with the double doors open. He pressed a button raising the giant antennae on the top of the truck. "Listen," I hollered before the news reporter said a word, "stay off the mother's property, she instructed me she would sign a compliant if anyone sets foot on it."

The lady reporter assured me, "I'm just here to do a live feed from the street. Is there any comment from the police department?'

I stared her straight in the eye, "no comment."

The man holding the camera said to the reporter, "I don't think we can use that?"

I knew the mother was in no mood to talk to a reporter. And the rapport between the police and the news media has always been symbiotic. They write stories embarrassing the police and we give them the freeze (say nothing).

"You sure are sweet talker," Sam said.

"And your shirt doesn't have enough dirt on it, so let's get back to searching."

Sam and I returned to the search area and looked under every rock with no results. I was thinking maybe we would have to expand the search area when the dispatcher announced, "beat 3322 come in."

"Go ahead dispatch," I responded.

"The canine unit you requested is at the house, he found the missing girl."

Who? How? What happened? My mind was racing a mile a minute. I literally ran back to the house. Sure enough, on the front lawn was the little girl with the pony tail in her mother's arm.

The mother looked at me and said "Thank You."

"You're welcome," I responded, although I had no idea for what.

The canine officer, holding the leash of a German Shepard, was standing off to the side. I motioned for him to come over to Sam and me. "O.K.," I said, "what did I miss?"

With a smirk on his face and a look of superiority, the canine officer answered "I found the girl."

"I can see that, but where?"

"In the house."

"What house?" I responded.

For some reason the canine officer was getting some satisfaction from dragging this out. Finally, he filled in the details. "I arrived about ten minutes ago and the mother told me the story. So I grabbed a few of the dolls in the yard the girl was playing with and let the dog sniff them. The dog sniffed the dolls and went directly back to the girl's house. Thinking he was tracking the girl's smell from earlier today, I pulled the dog away from the house. But he kept pulling back to the house and scratched at the door. The mother opened the door and the dog went directly to the little girl's room and sniffed under the bed and sat down. As you know the dog is trained to sit when he finds what he is searching for. So I looked under the bed and there was the girl."

What was she doing under the bed?" Sam asked.

*D.R. Novak*

The mother walked over upon overhearing our conversation. "That would be my fault. I taught Sarah how to play 'hide and go seek' last week and, for some reason, she sneaked past me while I was on the phone and hid under the bed." Apologetically, the mother continued, "I'm really sorry about this."

"I'm glad she's fine . . . that's all that matters," Sam assured the mother.

I got on the radio and tried to undo everything that was done. "Dispatch, thank everyone for the assist. The girl was found unharmed, call off the search."

Walking back to the car while dodging the news reporter, Sam chimed in, "we tied up 4 cars, a marine unit, a helicopter, and a canine unit to search for a girl that was in her own house."

I gazed over at Sam and said, "I won't tell the sergeant if you don't."

# CHAPTER 9

## The stolen car

Every day the police have to make split second decisions on the street. At times those decisions can be the difference between life and death. Sam and I were about to make a big decision: where to go for lunch. On the surface, this may seem easy, but taking into account the quality of the food, the ambience of the restaurant and the service provided is not easy. Actually, only one factor determines our lunch location: police discount. Some places are fifty-percent off and some are free. Several ideas were bantered about as I was driving in circles. Pulling behind a Chevrolet stopped at the light, I noticed the car was the same make, model and color as Sam's car. How could I not have noticed? Sam had brought the car right off the assembly line two weeks ago. He talks about it like it's one of his children. I nudged Sam who was daydreaming out the window, "hey, look, that guy has the same car as you do."

Sam stared at the car and squinted at the license plate. "That's not a car like mine . . . that is mine . . . that's my license plate number."

I couldn't tell if Sam was kidding or not, "are you yanking my chain?"

Sam pulled his gun from the holster and pointed it out the window at the car. "STOP THAT CAR," he shouted.

I turned on the emergency lights and siren. Sam's car accelerated quickly through the red light and pulled away. I hesitated for a moment, "your car got some nice pick-up, Sam." Then I punched the gas pedal and the chase was on. The vehicle made a hard right turn down a residential street. He was no dummy—if he was going to lose the police, he knew he would have to hit the less traveled side streets and alleys hoping to lose us. The squad car was not a mechanical marvel and struggled to keep up with Sam's car. As we got within a hundred yards, Sam aimed and fired. POP.POP.

Over the noise of the engine I yelled, "you know you're shooting at your own car?" But Sam didn't care; he leveled the gun again. POP. POP.

In the mist of the chaos, two thoughts crossed my mind. First, it is against Department policy to engage in a vehicle pursuit to stop a stolen car. It seems counter-productive, but several previous vehicle chases in the past resulted in horrific traffic accidents in which innocent bystanders were killed. The city got sued and paid through the nose in punitive damages. In all of those cases, the police vehicle was not involved in the accident, only the fleeing vehicle. But the lawyer, knowing the city has the deep pockets, goes after the city. I'm not a lawyer (Shakespeare was right) but case law says the city is responsible for the actions of a third party (the fleeing offender). If you were not chasing him he would not speed to get away and hurt someone. It's a twisted world we live in. And, secondly, shooting at a vehicle is against Department policy. To make matters worse, since we cannot officially chase the suspect, we cannot call the chase in over the radio and ask for assistance.

Sam's car continued at a high rate of speed down another residential street. He hit a corner hard and overturned the wheel throwing the car into a skid. The car fish-tailed several times before jumping the curb. The driver regained control and continued down the block on the sidewalk. Staying as close as I could Sam reached out the window again and fired at the back of the car. POP. POP. The driver seemed inexperienced at the wheel and I figured it was only a matter of time before he lost control. It was a catch-22. If he smashed the car, he would be caught and Sam would get his car back in pieces. If he got away, the car would be in one piece, but gone. Reaching the end of the block the car turned hard again—too hard. The front right tire blew and the car rocked back and forth.

"He's loosing it," I screamed at Sam.

The car teetered back and forth on its frame. The driver's door swung open as the car started losing speed from the drag of the flat tire. While still moving, the driver jumped from the vehicle and went into a roll as the car's momentum pushed him forward. Watching the driver break out of his roll and get up running, I did not pay any attention to my squad car; it was still moving at a fast clip and coming up fast on Sam's car that had now come to stop.

"Watch out," Sam shouted.

I slammed on the brakes and the wheels locked (no Anti-lock braking systems on these cars). "This is going to be close," as I braced for impact. The bald tires strained and the squad car jerked to a halt about a foot from the Sam's bumper. As I let out an exhale, Sam was already exiting the car and chasing the driver. I looked down the block to see the subject, about a 17 year old kid, high jump a four foot fence without breaking stride. Sam was trying to catch up and running faster than I ever saw him move before—this was personal. Sam reached the four foot fence and tried to emulate the young kids move by leaping over. He almost made it, stressing the word almost. As he jumped his front foot cleared the fence and I thought for a second he was going to make it, but his back foot clipped the top of the fence and Sam went into a tumble. He hit the pavement awkward and remained motionless. I ran over to check on my partner.

"Sam, you O.K.?"

Sam slowly got up, "only my ego is hurt."

As we walked back to the squad car, the dispatcher called, "beat 3322."

"Talk about bad timing," I said to Sam. "Go ahead, dispatch."

"We are receiving several calls of 'shots fired' in the area of 135th and Clifton."

Sam raised his hand and smiled. "That would be me."

"We'll get right on that dispatch," I answered in a serious tone.

Sam did a quick inspection of his vehicle. Aside from the flat tire the only other damage to the vehicle was the ignition switch was busted caused by starting the car without a key. Considering the high-speed chase we had, I would consider that a victory. Sam got his key out and opened the trunk of his car to remove the spare.

"Let's do this fast," I told Sam, "before someone takes down our car number and beefs about you shooting your gun out the car window."

Moving quickly, Sam and I worked in unison like a pit crew on the Indy 500 race track. Sam jacked the car up while I loosened the lug nuts. As soon as the tire cleared the ground Sam was already rolling the spare into place. I tightened the bolts as Sam dropped the car. He threw the damaged tire and spare into trunk and he was off. I followed with the squad car back to the station house.

In the parking lot of the station I met back up with Sam and popped the trunk release for the squad car. Sam pulled out a small box and jumped in the squad car. The small box contained all the necessary tools to clean Sam's gun. He field stripped the pistol (taking the slide off) and cleaned the gun with solvent. A few drops of oil were added to lubricate it before putting the gun back together; it literally took two minutes. Why the rush? In case some good citizen (I'm being facetious) did witness Sam shoot his gun and called to complain. In that event, the sergeant would be required to do an immediate investigation, which meant examining Sam's gun to see if it was fired. With the gun as clean as the day he bought it, there would be no smell of gunpowder or powder residue in the barrel.

After the gun was cleaned and we were home free I said to Sam," that takes a lot guts to come into a police lot and steal a car right out from under our noses."

"But why did it have to be my car," Sam gasped.

"Like we tell everyone we do an auto theft report for—that's what insurance is for."

Sam nodded in a final act of acceptance.

Seeing that Sam was now calm, I figured I would take one jab at him. "You know, for guy who brags he is such a great shot, I didn't see one bullet hole in the back of your car. How could you miss as object as big as a car with six shots?"

Without missing a beat, Sam glanced over at me and said, "missed . . . never . . . all six shots must have gone up the exhaust pipe."

# CHAPTER 10

# Here kitty-kitty

It seems bad things do come in threes. The first call today concerned a woman who wanted to report a suspicious object. When we arrived the woman said she saw an Unidentified Flying Object (UFO). We told her since the aircraft was not on our beat there was nothing we could do. We don't have inter-galactic jurisdiction. She wanted our badge numbers and said she was going to report us (I was afraid to ask who she would report us to). I'm sure the fact she was heavily medicated and recently released from a mental institution had nothing to do with it.

The second call involved a man who wanted his next door neighbor arrested. It was windy that day and the neighbor's tree fell on his house, putting a big crease in his roof. Sam explained it's not a crime and there was nothing we could do, however, the man persisted. Sam finally said, "I'll meet you half way . . . I'll arrest the tree." The man was not amused and asked for our badge numbers; he wanted to report us.

Then call number three comes from the dispatcher: "See the woman about a cat in the tree . . . animal control will meet you there."

The powers-that-be on the department decided a long time ago that it is good community relations for the police to respond to all calls for service—no matter how ridiculous. If someone wants the police, they get the police.

Sam was not in the best of moods today and I knew this call was not going to improve his disposition. I stayed silent as Sam drove toward the address. I learned many moons ago it was best to stay out of his way when he was in one of those 'every citizen is an idiot' state of mind. Approaching the scene, Sam hit the emergency lights and increased his speed. I had no idea what he was doing—and I didn't want to know. Ahead, I could see a woman standing on her front lawn in a house coat with curlers in her hair.

"You are going too fast," I warned Sam.

Sam kept the speed up until we were about 100 feet from the lady. Seeing no cars parked at the curb, Sam locked the brakes intentionally throwing the car into a skid. The right front tire hit the curb, bounced off, then struck it again. The tires, pinching the curb, made a loud screeching noise similar to fingernails on a chalkboard before coming to a rest pinned against the curb.

Sam pounced from the car and headed for the lady. Her jaw was wide open after witnessing Sam's arrival. "Where's the cat burglar?" he asked. The lady, still trying to recover from our arrival, began stammering, no . . . cat . . . burglar . . . only . . . cat."

Laughing inside, I asked the lady, "where is the cat?"

The lady pointed up to an over grown dog wood tree on the front lawn (yes, a cat in a dog tree). The tree stretched about 40 feet high. And, of course, on the very last limb at the top of the tree was a brown tabby cat. The cat was sitting still staring down, as if taunting us. To make matters worse, due to Sam's vaudeville arrival, several neighbors came out of their houses to see what the commotion was all about; the crowd encircled us.

"Just a cat in the tree," I assured everyone.

The crowd lingered around as Sam and I waited for an animal control officer to arrive. I thought about calling the fire department, but the tree branches near the top were quite small and frail and would not support a ladder. When the animal control officer arrived, he met us under the tree. He was carrying a four foot catch pole. The pole had an open claw on one end with a cable running up the pole to the handle. Squeezing the handle closed the jaws. The animal control officer, I'm guessing about 40 years old and out of shape, was not going to have an easy time scaling that tree. I guess he knew that too, as he addressed me and my partner: "I'm not going up that tree."

Sam, already incensed about being here, said "that's your job."

"Catching animals is my job," the officer explained, "not climbing trees. Anyway, I'm afraid of heights."

By now I could smoke coming out of Sam's ears. Sam pulled the gun from his holster and stated "I'll get the cat down."

The whole crowd let out a gasp. But Sam handed the gun to me and said "hold this . . . I'm going up." He grabbed the catch pole from the officer's hand and made his way toward the tree. Sam was in good shape, but I had a bad feeling about this. I opined, "maybe we better come up with a better plan."

"I got this," Sam replied as he lifted his leg to climb the tree.

I watched as Sam made his way up the tree. The tree trunk split into two smaller stumps about ten feet up and Sam was able to wedge his foot in between the two stumps to maintain balance. As Sam continued up he was able to position his foot between the center tree trunk and smaller trunks branching off until he reached the top. Once at the top, Sam reached out with the catch pole but the pole was not long enough. He would have to precariously step away from the trunk of the tree and onto a small branch. Moving slowly, he ventured out on the branch until the cat was within reach. As he reached for the cat, the limb snapped and the cat and Sam started their descent. Snapping off several branches on the way down the cat hit the ground first. Under the tree was a bed of flowers in soft dirt that cushioned the cat's fall. Sam fell horizontally, face down, and locked his elbows to break his fall. He landed in the same soft patch of dirt as the cat. After hitting the ground he rolled away from the tree and right over the cat. The cat let out a high-pitch sound that had the potential to bust every window on the block.

I rushed to Sam's side. The cat owner, the crowd and the animal control officer rushed over to the cat's side. I thought that spoke volumes of the how the citizens we serve care about us. Looking down at Sam I asked, "you hurt, partner?"

"I'll be fine," Sam moaned.

I directed my attention over to the cat. He looked like he was steamrolled by Sam. I thought if that cat had nine lives Sam knocked it down to eight. But the cat was moving, which I took as a good sign. The cat owner kept repeating "My poor baby, my poor baby," as the crowd tried to console her. The animal control officer gently picked the cat up and carried him over to the truck. He opened a rear compartment used to house stray animals and laid the cat down. He rushed to the front, and, from the passenger seat, retrieved a small medical bag.

The officer removed a small IV bag from the medical kit and hooked it on a latch above the cat. He then inserted a needle into the cat's paw. Still working feverishly, he removed a small oxygen tank and mask from the medical bag. He quickly slipped the mask over the cat's ears and over his mouth.

'I'm glad someone is getting medical attention, Sam remarked loudly.

But, aside from me, no one was paying attention to Sam. I helped Sam up from the ground and dusted him off. "Let's get out of here," I told Sam.

The animal control officer informed the cat owner he needed to take the cat back to the shelter for medical care. He assured the lady he would do everything he could to save the cat.

Before Sam and I could reach the car the cat owner warned us, "You will pay for this, I'm an important person in this community."

Usually I was the steady hand over Sam in situations like this but I was getting irate too. My partner went out his way to try and help and that's the thanks we get. I responded, "I could tell you are important by that house coat and curlers you are wearing."

"I want your badge numbers," she yelled back.

"And I want total consciousness, but we don't always get what we want now do we," I stated.

Sam had already started the car and put in gear as I jumped in fast. Pulling away I looked at Sam and mentioned, "it's a hat trick . . . that's the third person who wanted our badge numbers today . . . and the day is still young." I gazed over at Sam who was still visually upset. He didn't say a word. I couldn't resist and asked, "what, cat got your tongue?"

# CHAPTER 11

## Off-duty

Being the police affords many benefits from free food to discounts at several retailers. One of the biggest perks is professional courtesy—police don't give other police officers parking or traffic tickets. In our city, the police union distributes to every officer a police medallion that affixes to the rear of their personal vehicle. The medallion signifies the vehicle belongs to a police officer and is given special treatment. Each medallion has a serial number on it like an officer's badge number. Before you start with the 'that's not fair speech,' let me remind every reader that most professions do the same for their members. Doctors take care of doctors, and lawyers take care of lawyers, and so forth down the line.

However, there is one situation where being the police has no advantage. While patrolling our beat, Sam and I got the call every police officer hates the most: "beat 3322, handle the disturbance at a bar involving an off-duty police officer. Beat 3320 (sergeant) will meet you there."

I cringed. The last thing a cop wants to do is arrest another cop. Any call where an off-duty officer is present requires that a Sergeant also respond. The reason being an off-duty officer does not have to listen to Sam and me because—well, he's the police too, he can tell me and my partner to go to hell. But he has to listen to a Sergeant who is a superior officer. Failing to obey a Sergeant's order results in formal charges for disobeying a direct order and that can get you fired.

Sam expressed my sentiment best. "I hope it's nobody we know."

Arriving at the location, the sergeant was parked in front waiting for us; he did not look happy. The tavern was a small dive with a neon beer sign flickering in the window. "Dam, I hate these calls," the Sergeant muttered as we headed for the door. The lighting inside was dim but I could see the outline of a large man sitting on the first barstool near the door. I immediately recognized him; it was Joe, an officer from the midnight shift. Looking past Joe I squinted to see several patrons cowering at the other end of the long bar. Behind the bar was a man waving his hands hysterically. Either he was trying to a land a plane or wanted my attention. As my eyes focused to the low light, the man pointed to the Joe and then to the back of the bar.

Sad nudged me. "Check out the juke box."

At the back of the bar was a free standing juke box with a bubble top. The top was made of glass with a large hole in it. I'm guessing the hole probably matched the size of Joe's fist. Joe was big. Not big as in fat, but big as in 200 pounds of muscle. His hands looked like bear claws and his arms were as big as my legs.

"Hi Joe," the sergeant said as he eased in Joe's direction, "what's going on?"

Joe never took his eyes off his beer in front of him and said "my wife left me today and somebody starting playing our song on the juke box. That's when I lost it."

Sam, probably out of curiosity, and trying to buy some time, asked, "what song was that, Joe?"

"Bad boys, bad boys—the theme song from cops."

How romantic I thought.

Inching closer, the sergeant added "let's go down to the station and talk this over."

While Joe was drunk he knew 'let's go down to the station' is code for you are about to get arrested. I could see Joe's muscles tense up. It was the classic fight or flight syndrome. And I knew it was the former.

Sam whispered to me, "should I call for back-up?"

I shook my head back and forth. I didn't know if Sam and I, along with the sergeant, could get handle Joe, but I did know more police would only antagonize Joe. Besides, too many officers can make arresting someone more difficult. Past experience has taught me that when a melee starts you are more likely to get elbowed, punched and kicked accidently from a fellow officer then the guy you are fighting.

The sergeant moved in closer and tried one more time. "We're your friends Joe, I need to come with us."

Joe wasn't buying it. The sergeant tried to grab Joe by the arm and Joe flicked his wrist causing the sergeant to stumble backward. Regaining his balance, the sergeant pushed forward as Sam and I circled around to either side. Just my luck, I was wearing a new pair of pants today and they were about to get dirty. The sergeant grabbed Joe by the wrist. Suddenly, Joe bent over and picked the sergeant up and lifted him over his head. He started turning in a circle and the sergeant looked like a spinning blade on a helicopter. I felt dizzy seeing the sergeant rotate. Sam and I tried to help the sergeant but we kept ducking to avoid getting hit by the sergeant's arm as they flew by, then by the sergeant's legs as they flew by, then by the arms again, and so on and so on. Joe grew tired of the helicopter imitation and threw the sergeant over the bar. A loud crash was heard as the sergeant was swallowed up behind the bar. With his back to me I lunged forward and landed on Joe's back. I wrapped my arms around Joe's neck as Sam went for the wrist and tried to put a handcuff on, but Joe would have none of it. He kicked Sam in the stomach sending him to the floor. Joe broke my grip around his neck and reached around and pulled me off his back. He turned toward me and raised me in the air by my forearms. With a quick heave of his arms I was airborne and traveling away from Joe at the speed of light. Einstein's theory is true: the faster you travel time does slow. For me, it seemed like time had stopped for a moment as everything seemed surreal. That's when another theory hit me: Newton's theory of gravity—what goes up must come down. I landed on the jukebox smashing through the already broken glass and then falling to the floor. Getting up slowly, the bartender then said to me, "who is going to pay for that jukebox?" I wanted to spout off a long list of expletives but now was not the time.

As I brushed chards of glass from my uniform, the sergeant emerged from behind the bar and was helping Sam as they both struggled with Joe. That's when the word of my old high-school coach resonated in my brain—"the easiest way to tackle a big guy is to hit him low." While Sam and the sergeant continued the fight, I darted toward the back of Joe with all my weight and threw my body at the back of Joe's knees. Joe's knees buckled and he fell backwards. There was only one flaw in my plan: Joe landed on top of me. My back ached and the compression on my back from Joe's weight made it difficult for me to suck in oxygen. But like a beached whale, Joe lost all his leverage while flopping on the floor on top of me. Sam was able to get one handcuff on Joe's left wrist and the sergeant got a handcuff of Joe's right wrist. Meeting in the middle, Sam and the sergeant linked the two handcuffs together. Meanwhile, I was slapping my open hand on the floor like a referee at a wrestling match trying to get Sam's attention. With Joe still on my back and no oxygen to speak, it was the only way to get Sam's attention. Seeing my distress, Sam rolled Joe off of me and asked, "You O.K. Partner?"

After taking a few deep breaths I replied "barely."

Sam went and talked to the bartender while I recovered. When Sam returned he filled me and the sergeant in: "The bartender is the owner. He says since none of the patrons were hurt, he would drop the charges if he was reimbursed for the damage to the jukebox—about 1,000 dollars."

The sergeant seemed to go along with the idea. "Let's take Joe in to the station, he suggested, before he beats up anymore machines."

We escorted Joe to an interrogation room in the station and handcuffed him to a bench. There, he turned from a belligerent drunk to a slobbering drunk. "I love you guys, "Joe said.

"And we love you," Sam insisted. While still inebriated, at least he no longer wanted to fight.

The watch commander, Captain Drew, heard the call on the radio and was looking for the Sam and me when we arrived at the station house. "Get in my office," he barked." Sam and I trailed the Captain into the watch commander's office where our sergeant was waiting for us. The Captain slammed the door closed. There we stood lined up covered in dirt with our uniforms tore like a rag-tag group of soldiers who fought a war—and lost.

"I want it straight," Captain Drew demanded, "what happened?" The Captain was a fair man but not known to bend the rules. He came from a police family. His grandfather, now retired, was a deputy chief and his father is a commander. He certainly rose through the ranks fast because of political connections (clout trumps merit in this city) and he had his eye on moving up. He wasn't going to risk his neck for Joe or any other officer.

This time Sam and I deferred to rank and let the sergeant talk. The sergeant started, "we brought Joe in for breaking a glass jukebox—it could have been an accident, we are still investigating."

Standing there dripping dirt on the rug I couldn't have been more proud of my sergeant for not throwing Joe under the bus. True, I might have internal injuries and I'm out two hundred bucks for a uniform, but having Joe arrested and costing him his job and pension was something I did not want conscience—and neither did Sam or the sergeant. Of course the Captain knew it was a bull, but he wasn't there to disprove it.

"Geez," the captain lectured, "it looks like the three of you were playing with mud pies. How did that happen?"

"Bad hygiene," I answered.

"Don't be a smart-ass. You know the procedure," the captain informed us, "he's going to have to blow the box."

The box is the breathalyzer machine. This is the point where being the police works against you. In any other profession, what you do with your free time is nobody else's business. But when you are the police, you are considered the police 24 hours a day and are held to a higher standard. Being drunk off-duty is considered conduct unbecoming an officer and subjects the officer to disciplinary action, up to and including firing.

The Captain went on. "A technician is on the way to the station to administer the test. Keep an eye on Joe until he gets her."

"Leaving the office, Sam frowned, "there is no way Joe can pass a sobriety test?"

"We got some time . . . I got an idea," I assured Sam.

The breathalyzer can only be administered by an officer who is specially trained and certified by the State to operate the machine. While waiting for this technician to arrive it is the responsibility of the officers to watch the drunk to make sure he does not eat or drink anything for at least 20 minutes prior to the test being administered. Any food or drink can alter the test results. Sam Kept an eye on Joe while I headed down the block to the convenience store to purchase some items and rushed back. Carrying a brown paper bag I returned through the back entrance making sure the Captain did not see me.

Ducking into the interrogation room where Sam was waiting, I spread the contents of the bag onto the table. It included a box of donuts, a bag of twinkies, a large slurpee, a pack of gum and a pack of cigarettes.

Sam smiled. "I see where you are going with this."

For the next 20 minutes Sam and I stuffed everything we could down Joe's throat. And Joe did not seem to mind. Speaking from experience, drunks always have an appetite (called the munchies). Just then, the sergeant peeked in the room to see how Joe was doing. Joe was sitting there with powered donut crumbs and slurpee juice on his shirt while chewing gum and a lit cigarette dangling from the corner of his mouth. The sergeant quickly closed the door and left—never to return.

We cleaned Joe up in time for the technician to arrive. The technician rolled in the breathalyzer machine that looked ancient (the station still has rotary phones). The machine looked like a control panel with buttons and knobs all over it with a long hollow tube attached to the side. The technician parked the machine next to Joe and placed a plastic mouthpiece on the end of the long tube, handed it to Joe and said, "blow until you hear a beep." Joe pressed his lips against the mouthpiece and exhaled as hard as he could into the tube. The machine beeped and we waited for the results. A minute later a thin strip of paper similar to a cash register receipt ejected from a slot on the front of the machine. The reading on the paper can be anywhere from 0.00 (no evidence of alcohol) to as high as numbers go (the highest I have ever seen was 2.40 which is pretty much alcohol poisoning and death). I crossed my fingers. The technician studied the slip and then looked at Joe. "We are going to have to try this again," he informed Joe. A new mouthpiece was inserted on the hose and Joe blew again. The technician studied the piece of paper and looked befuddle. He showed me the slip. It read MALFUNCTION . . . CALL FOR SERVICE. Inside I was jumping up and down. The combination of carbohydrates, sugar, caffeine, and nicotine flowing through Joe's body confused the machine. The technician left the room and Sam and I high-fived each other.

Before we could continue our celebration, the Captain stormed into the room. "What did you guys do to the machine?"

Sam, with a devious smile on his face, said "I don't know what you mean, Captain."

The Captain took a breath and seemed to calm down. Lowering his voice, he said, "even if the bar owner will not press charges and the breathalyzer cannot prove Joe is drunk, I can't let him walk out of here, what if he does something else stupid today, it could mean my badge."

"You have my word Captain," I pleaded, "I can guarantee that Joe will go home and sleep it off."

For the first time since knowing the Captain his face appeared indecisive. Struggling to get the words out he finally said, "get him out of here."

Before he could change his mind Sam and I had Joe in the backseat of the squad car heading toward Joe's house. While Sam was working the cell phone arranging a fundraising party for Joe to replace the jukebox, I followed Joe into his house and put him to bed. Returning to the squad car Sam asked, "what if he decides to start drinking again and goes back out, you promised the Captain he would stay home?"

"That reminds me," I answered Sam, "we have to stop by Joe's tomorrow morning."

"Why is that?"

"To un-handcuff Joe from his bed."

# CHAPTER 12

# With this ring

It was a long eight hours and Sam was driving toward the station when he quickly braked. I lifted my head to see a woman by the curb waving for us to stop. I gave Sam a hard stare; he knew stopping for hand wavers is the Holy Grail of no-no's on this job. The first thing you learn on the street is handle your radio calls and don't go looking for problems—it's called driving with blinders on. "You had to do it," I chastised Sam.

Sam shrugged his shoulder, "sorry partner, hitting the brakes was a reflex action." By now the woman was pounding on the window and we had no choice. I rolled down my window. "What's the problem," I asked.

"A couple is having an argument in the apartment next to mine. It sounds really heated. They are disturbing the whole building."

"We'll handle it lady." Actually, I thought, Sam would handle it because he is the one who stopped. Sam parked the car and we made our way toward the apartment building. "You want the apartment number?" the woman inquired. "I'll just follow the noise," I answered. Walking into the lobby the loud shouting echoed off the walls. Sam looked up the stairway. "Sounds like the third floor," he guessed. There was an elevator but Sam and I never use them. Always being on guard, an elevator would be a perfect way to ambush any police arriving. If the doors open and someone is there with a gun there is nowhere to run and nowhere to hide. Drudging up three flights of stairs

65

we located the door the shouting was coming from. Sam took a position on one side of the door and me on the other. We stood there quietly for a moment to hear what was going on before knocking. It seems the woman was upset about the boyfriend not working, and the boyfriend was complaining about being disrespected. We heard enough and Sam wrapped on the door with his knuckles. The apartment grew quiet as footsteps approached the door. "Who that?"

"Police," Sam announced.

"I didn't call any police."

"Your neighbors did, open the door."

The door slowly opened and a man with a sleeveless T-shirt and jeans stood there with a nervous expression. Sam pushed the door further open and we entered the apartment. "We don't need the police," the man insisted.

"Where is the other half of 'we'," I asked.

"My girlfriend is in the kitchen."

Sam made his way to the back of the apartment to check on the woman. For all we knew she was dead or tied up. The living room was sparsely furnished with an old coach and a coffee table. What the apartment lacked in furniture was offset in cockroaches—they were everywhere. There were so many cockroaches crawling up and down the wall it looked like the wall paper was moving. Sam and I have been in apartments with cockroaches before and the trick is to prevent them from crawling up your leg. Once they find a home in your pants, you become a carrier. And carrying them back to the squad car can infest the vehicle. Or worst yet, carrying them home in your clothes can infest your house. The trick is to keep your feet moving so the buggers can't latch on to you. Even while standing in place it is important to keep raising one foot of the floor then the other—like marching in place.

Trying to keep an eye on Sam with my peripheral vision I asked the man several questions. Moving the conversation quickly I learned the man's name is Jack and he has been having a hard time finding a job. He feels bad because they recently had a baby and cannot support them. Sam returned with a young woman carrying a newborn in her arms. She was upset and directed her anger at the boyfriend: "you don't love me anymore and disappear for days at a time."

He answered, "I told you I would marry you . . . I just don't have the money now."

Thinking this argument could on for hours with no resolution in sight, it was time to speed the process along. "Listen," I told both of them, "how about we get you two married right now?"

The woman face looked startled, "how can we get married now?"

"A police officer is like a captain of the ship" as I pointed to the badge on my chest, "we have certain powers."

"What kind of powers?" the woman asked.

"I can notarize any document you have or perform the marriage ceremony."

Sam smirked as he shuffled his feet.

I continued marching in place and positioned the couple next to each other with the baby sandwiched in between. Before either one figured what was going on I figured I could have a little ceremony and get the hell out of there as the cockroaches were circling. Anyway, with the thought of getting married, the two seemed to forget all about the fight.

"What's your name I asked the woman?"

She answered, "Jill."

"All right, Jill . . . do you take Jack to be your husband and promise to cut him some slack while he looks for a job?"

Standing there like a glowing bride, she replied "I do."

"And do you, Jack, promise to take Jill as you wife and not disappear for days?"

"I guess so," Jack answered.

Jill interrupted. "A ring, how can we get married without a ring?"

Sam reached into his pocket and removed an elastic band and handed it to me. I wrapped it around Jill's finger. "This will be the ring."

Jill studied the piece of elastic and said, "it's a rubber band."

"Rubber band . . . wedding band it's all the same. It is the thought that counts. By the authority vested in me by the State I now pronounce you man and wife. Kiss the bride. We got to go."

Sam and I dodged a few more cockroaches and scampered toward the door.

"Wait," Jill called out, "what about a marriage certificate?"

Sam reached into his pocket and pulled out an unused crumpled report and a pen. He crossed out the words 'arrest report' and scribbled 'marriage certificate.' "There you go, "Sam explained, "just scratch out the word offender #1 and put your name in and scratch out the word offender #2 and put your husband's name in."

Like a flash Sam and I were out of the apartment and down the steps. At the bottom of the landing we checked each other's pants leg—no cockroaches.

Walking to the car Sam mentioned "maybe now, thinking they are married, they might stop fighting."

"How could it not work out," I stated emphatically, "with a name like Jack and Jill it has to be a story book ending."

# CHAPTER 13

# The Stand-Off

It was a frigid day and Sam was either nodding off in the passenger seat or passed out from carbon monoxide poisoning. The squad car leaked exhaust fumes so we had to drive with the windows open, and, of course, the heater did not work. The engine kept making a strange knocking noise and the engine light on the dashboard has been illuminated all day. The steering pulled one direction than the other, but always in the direction of the junk yard; it knew.

Another squad car was on the radio about chasing a stolen car. A little while ago a woman stopped for gas and left the car running. Someone seized the opportunity to go for a permanent test drive. The shouting on the radio awoke Sam. "What's going on?" Sam wanted to know while wiping the sandman from his eyes.

"Beat 3344 is chasing a stolen car, a black Honda, but it is all the way on the other side of the district—way too far for us to get involved." And it was just a matter of time before the sergeant will call off the chase anyway. The streets are too slick with patches of frost—high speed chases and ice don't mix. Trying to think like the criminal element (which hurts my head) it occurred to me most criminals with a stolen car try to make the expressway. On the open road, they quickly leave our jurisdiction and are home free.

The expressway was only about a mile away so I headed in that direction. Nearing the entrance ramp I could see a car fast approaching in the rear view mirror. "It couldn't be," I informed Sam.

Sam turned his neck around to look. "I think it is," he shouted, "block the ramp."

I pulled the squad car perpendicular to the entrance ramp blocking the roadway. The car approached and turned toward us like it was going to get on the ramp one way or another. Sam reached for and buckled his seatbelt. I did the same. If we were about to get T-boned I figured we had a better chance surviving inside the car. The car continued straight as arrow for us. "Brace yourself" Sam called out. As the car got close enough to read the front plate the driver must have changed his mind. He veered to the right and the car fishtailed. The back swung around and sideswiped the side of the squad car with a thunderous boom. The stolen vehicle rebounded of the squad car and sped off. I hit the gas as the squad car sputtered forward. This was going to be the shortest chase in history, I thought, as the squad car lagged behind. That's when we caught a break. The driver, not familiar with the area, turned into an alley, probably trying to double back to the expressway ramp. But the alley was a dead-end and he skidded to a halt at a brick wall.

"Get ready for a foot chase," I cautioned Sam in anticipation of the usual bailout from the car. But as I pulled onto the rear bumper of the car the driver did not move. He made no attempt to get out of the car. Sam and I looked at each other in amazement. "He knows were here," Sam stated.

"Thanks for that news flash, partner. Maybe he's waiting for an invitation. Let's go get him."

I walked up to the driver's side with my gun trained at the back of the driver's head. Sam came up from the passenger side with his gun out also. What worried me most was that the stolen car was still running. What if he threw the car in reverse and tried to push the squad car back up the alley? Creeping slowly to the driver's door, I could see inside. The driver looked like a young boy, no more than 15 years of age. His hands were gripping the steering wheel so tight his knuckles were white; he was spooked. I holstered my gun and pressed my face against the glass. "Open the door," I hollered.

The driver removed his hands from the steering wheel and gazed over at me. He folded his arms over one another in an act of defiance and shook his head no. Basically, we had a young kid behind the wheel of a stolen car throwing a temper tantrum. "Now what," Sam asked.

"We could wait him out, but he's sitting in a nice warm car with the heater on and we are standing outside."

"How about shooting the window out," Sam suggested.

"Too risky." The ammunition the department gives us is low grain (not much gun powder) and hollow point (soft lead bullets). These bullets are prone to bounce off things, even glass, and head in unpredictable directions. The department is more concerned about liability then officer safety. A high powered bullet offers more stopping power, but if the shot misses its target that bullet could hit somebody a mile away and the lawyers would have a field day with that. I thought of breaking the window, but the new safety glass is shatterproof and very difficult to smash. Then it hit me as the little delinquent was sitting nice and toasty in the car with the heat on. I reached for my canister of mace from my gun belt and leaned over the hood of the vehicle. Searching with my eyes I located vents secreted under the front edge of the hood below the windshield. These intake vents are present on all cars and pull fresh air from the outside. The air is then sent through a heater core where it is warmed and then inside the vehicle. Putting the nozzle of the mace against the vents I emptied the whole can into the vents.

Sam watched what I was doing and nodded his approval. "This ought to be good," he predicted. The mace we carry is a 10-percent solution of pepper spray made entirely of hot peppers. Inhaling the fumes from the aerosol immediately causes severe burning sensation to the skin and a burning of the eyes. Because it is all natural ingredients, the effect is short (about 10 minutes) and causes no permanent damage. Sam and I didn't have to wait long. After a few minutes the vehicle started to fill with mace. The youngster face turned red and he began gagging. He tried holding his breath, but the effort was futile. I could see liquid streaming out of his nose as the nostrils were irritated and his eyes watered. Surprisingly, he sat there and still refused to open the door.

"What next," Sam asked.

Getting a little agitated I walked to the trunk of the squad car. No little kid is going to get the best of my, I thought. Returning with a jack handle I walked up to the window and waved the object at the kid. "Open the door or else" I yelled. The youngster still refused to give up. "You asked for it," I warned him.

Sam said, "I don't think that will break the window."

"I'm not going to break the window . . . watch and learn, "I instructed Sam.

I advanced to the front of the vehicle between the front bumper and the wall. Feeling through the front grill of the car with my hand I found what I was hunting for. With the jack handle in my hand I wound up like a pitcher ready to throw a fastball. Using all my might, I swung the handle down into the grill of the car. I looked at kid in the car . . . nothing. I wound up and hit the grill again. This time I hit the mark and a loud burst erupted inside the vehicle. Both air bags deployed. I had found the crash sensor on the front of the vehicle that deployed the airbags. The driver's airbag caught the kid by surprise and slapped him in the face. A white powder from the airbag filled the compartment and seemed to hang in the air. Mixing with the residue of the mace it almost looked like snow storm in vehicle.

Sam observed: "remember those snow globes filled with white powder and water we used to shake as kids?"

I let out a big laugh. "That's exactly what it resembled. But more importantly, it did the trick. The youngster opened the door and fell out of the car. Sam quickly handcuffed him. From the mace and the airbag powder he didn't look too healthy laying there. His face was white as a ghost and he twisted his neck around as he began projectile vomiting.

"Think he needs medical attention?" Sam asked.

"No . . . I think he needs an exorcism."

# CHAPTER 14

## Juveniles

"Beat 3322 handle the call of tampering with the green auto at 14550 S. City Street, the complainant is anonymous." Nobody ever wants to talk the police in person, so most calls are anonymous. Seen talking to the police brands you a snitch and getting life insurance would be difficult, and the neighborhood around City Street is the worst of the worst. I carry a gun and badge and I don't go there after sunset unless called. About once a week Sam and I get a call of a person shot on City Street—it's always bona fide. We take our time reaching the destination because we know we are only going to pick up the body. Sam and I put up crime scene tape and loiter around waiting for the arrival of the medical examiner to remove the body. The people in the area take a peculiar enjoyment in seeing crime scenes. With the body covered in a sheet on the sidewalk people spill out of their houses with lawn chairs and gather around. It's like a big social event and people visit with each other. A small fast food joint in the area shows up with a hot dog cart. He's like a vendor at a baseball game shouting, "Hot dogs . . . burgers . . . peanuts . . . as he works the crowd. The joint listens to police calls on the police band and shows up at all crime scenes.

I rolled up on the location and didn't see any green auto parked in front. The car was probably gone by now; it takes about 2 minutes for a bad auto thief to steal a car.

Sam suggested, "check around back."

The alley behind the address was under the elevated public train tracks. Turning off the squad car lights and inching down the alley, I weaved the car in and out of the steel girders that supported the trains. A train passed above throwing sparks from the metal wheels grinding along the steel tracks and making an ear piercing sounds that hurt my eardrums.

The train passed and I was getting ready to get the hell out of there when Sam howled "stop the car."

Depressing the brake I said, "I don't see anything."

Sam pointed to a green Buick parked next to a fence. As I drew a bead with my eyes I saw the topmost part of a forehead in the front seat of the green car. Sam loped from the vehicle toward the green car. The man in the car, seeing Sam coming, jumped out of the open window and ran away toward a gangway with Sam close behind. I gunned the engine and blew down the alley. I was too far behind Sam to help in the foot chase, but if I could make the corner and come back up the next block, maybe I could cut off the fleeing suspect. Waiting on the adjacent block I scanned the street—no shadows, no movement. Within a minute Sam appeared from then gangway. Catching his breath, Sam yelled, "Did you see him?"

"He never came out," I shouted back.

Sam turned back toward the gangway he exited and said, "he must have jumped some fences . . . he's laying down in some yard."

A standard trick of the criminal is to hide under back porches or run up some back stairway and lay flat until the police leave. Most police, when searching for a fleeing suspect, simply drive up and down the streets and alleys shining a spotlight in yards. The suspect figures he can remain in place and out-wait the police until they give up and leave. But if that was the suspect's thinking, he made a serious mistake. I parked the squad car, grabbed my flashlight and followed Sam back into the gangway. Reaching the backyard, Sam pointed east saying, "I'll start hopping fences this way and check yards, you go west partner."

"Holler if you see anything," I cautioned Sam as he flipped a fence. I thought about notifying the dispatcher what we were doing, but I didn't have any description of the suspect then a male in dark clothing. Also, I did not know why we were chasing him, other than running from the police. Many of times I have chased down suspects who ran when the saw police only to catch them and not know what they did. And, on every occasion, when I caught someone for running and asked "why you running?" the answer always came back "because you were chasing me." Then I would say "I can't chase you unless you run first." But the suspect would always insist "you chased me first." I guess it's like the chicken and egg argument.

Hopping fences I kept my eyes out for two things: the suspect and big dogs. I worked my way down about six houses with no luck when I heard Sam calling "over here." Backtracking over several fences I located Sam on the second floor of a rear porch pointing his gun down. On the ground was the suspect rolled up in a carpet. Sam watched the suspect at gunpoint while I unrolled the suspect and handcuffed him. Leading him back to the squad car I had to ask, "why did you run?"

"Because you were chasing me."

I was sorry I asked. I searched the suspect and found a student ID on him. He was 16 years old and in 9th Grade—a real go-getter.

Placing the suspect in the rear of the squad car Sam went over to investigate the green Buick. Giving it the once over, he waved me to join him. Training his flashlight on the steering column of the car I could see the damage. The plastic housing was peeled away and a long metal lever that went down the steering column was exposed. By pulling up on the lever the vehicle's ignition is bypassed and the car can be started without a key (newer cars have computer chips that prevent this).

"Look-ey here," Sam bragged, "we caught an auto thief in the act."

"Look-ey here," I mocked Sam, showing him the student ID, "he's only 16 years old." Until one reaches seventeen, he is considered a juvenile and a complete different set of laws apply. If he was seventeen he would be charged as an adult and would go straight to jail. Since auto theft is a felony he would be denied bail tonight and would have to see a judge tomorrow. In court, bail would be set and the suspect may or may not be able to post bail. But since he is only sixteen, a juvenile under the law, it's almost like a walk in the park. He will be taken to the station where a juvenile detective (called diaper detectives since they only deal with youths) takes custody of him and calls the parents in. The juvenile is then released to the parent and goes home immediately; it is almost a waste of time arresting him, he will be on his way home before Sam and I finish the paperwork. And gangs know this too, that's why juveniles hold drugs and guns for the gang. If they caught with the contraband they go home with the parents instead of to prison.

"A juvenile," Sam spouted as he snatched the ID from my hand and looked closely at it under his flashlight. Sam looked at me with a devious expression on his face. "Did you see the birthdate?" he quizzed me.

"What difference does that make? Based on the year he was born he is sixteen."

"You are losing your touch," Sam scolded me, "he was born on May 15th, and what day is today?"

Thinking for a moment, then it occurred to me—today is May 14th. I checked my watch; it was 2245 hours (10:45 P.M.) Now a devious smile crossed my face. He will be seventeen years old in one-hour-and-fifteen minutes. "I see where you are going with this partner, but what do we do with him for over an hour?" I asked Sam.

I could see the wheels had been turning in Sam's mind already. He answered, "lunch."

So with the juvenile handcuffed and strapped in with the seatbelt in the backseat, I drove to one of our favorite eating establishments for a bite to eat. On the way there Sam told the suspect he wasn't going to the station until after midnight, and then he would be charged as an adult. The suspect begged to be taken to the station immediately and charged as a juvenile. That's the first time someone pleaded with Sam and I to be charged with a crime quickly. I parked the squad car in front and grabbed a booth by the window. Sam and I ate a three course meal while I kept an eye on the suspect through the glass. After the meal Sam paid the discounted check and returned with a doggy bag in his hand.

"What's that for?" I asked Sam.

"I brought a little something for our guest in the squad car."

How nice, and unusual, I thought. Checking my watch it was 2358 hours (11:58 P.M.). I drove slowly to the station and arrived a little after midnight. We knocked out the paperwork and walked the suspect to the lock-up and into a cell with the other adult prisoners. Sam opened the bag he was carrying from the restaurant and removed a cupcake. The cupcake had frosting and sprinkles on it with a single candle sticking straight up. Sam lit the candle, handed it to the suspect and said "happy birthday."

# CHAPTER 15

## Car and driver

Sam pulled the squad car out of the police lot to start another fun-filled day when a car sped past. "No respect," Sam observed as the car rushed past the station. The Captain was on Sam and I about our ticket activity (or lack thereof) lately. Writing a ticket today and keeping the Captain happy seemed like it was in the cards. Sam activated the lights and pulled the driver over about four blocks from the station. The first thing I noticed was the car had a temporary license plate on the back. A temporary plate has numbers and letters like a permanent plate but is made of cardboard and is only valid for 30 days. It is issued for a new registration on a car until the paperwork is submitted to the Secretary of State's Office and permanent plates are issued.

The vehicle was a silver Mercedes Benz, about 5 years old, with no scratches or dents—pride of ownership was evident. I walked up to the driver's window and Sam watched from the rear. The driver, a black male, was alone and seemed nervous, although most people are nervous when they are stopped by the police. Nobody wants a traffic ticket and some apprehension is expected. In general, having contact with the police always brings a negative association. When you think about it, most good citizens meet the police one of two ways: they are the victim of a crime or stopped for a traffic violation—neither very pleasant.

Trying to reassure the driver, I smiled and said, "going a little fast there."

The driver made eye contact and smiled back. He replied, "I'm sorry officer, I got a lot of things on mind . . . I'm having a bad day."

I could relate to that. Since he was very polite and seemed like a nice guy, I was about to let him go when I heard Sam from the back of the car clear his throat loudly—either he was coming down with something or he wanted my attention.

"I'll be with you in a moment," I told the driver and walked to the rear of the car. Sam pointed down at the bumper but didn't say a word. I sensed he thought the car was stolen but did not want to alert the driver.

I walked back to the driver. Is this your car?"

"Yes sir, officer."

"How long have you owned the car?"

"About 5 years now."

So far so good I thought. "How come you have temporary plates if you had the car 5 years?"

"The plates were stolen about a week ago so I had to get the temporary ones until new plates are issued."

The answered seemed to roll off his tongue, and everything he said certainly sounded plausible. But it was then I knew Sam's hunch was right—the car was stolen. Playing along I said, "everything seems to be in order, I just need to see your driver's license."

The driver fumbled around for a few minutes checking his pockets then checking the passenger compartment and searching under the seat. "I'm so sorry, officer, I must have left it at home . . . I will be more careful in the future."

He was definitely killing me with kindness, and he dressed the part of a Mercedes Benz owner. Even while seated, I could see he was wearing tailored pants with a sharp crease down the leg, along with a dress shirt and matching tie. He dressed like he belonged on the cover of GQ (Gentle Men's Quarterly magazine).

"It will be just one more moment, sir."

I returned to the rear of the vehicle where Sam was talking over the radio with the dispatcher. He ran the license plate hoping for a registration for the owner. But the dispatcher told Sam what I already knew "no record." Since it was a temporary plate the registration (information about the owner of vehicle) would not be in the computer system yet.

"Any ideas?" Sam asked.

"I'm glad you asked, partner. I'll get him out of the car and you get the VIN (vehicle identification number) from the dashboard. Running that serial number should get a name and address of the owner."

Wearing a rut between the driver's vehicle and the squad car, I made my made to the driver's window again. "Can you step out of the car for me, sir." Since he was being polite I thought I would return the favor. "I don't want to detain you too long but I have to check if you have a valid license—kindly step to the squad car."

The man alighted from his vehicle and walked toward my car. I opened the back door for him and he took a seat. Since I couldn't prove the car was stolen I let him sit in the car without handcuffs. While I engaged the man in small talk, Sam ringed his away around to the front of the Mercedes and scratched down the VIN number. He got on the radio and waited for the registration information from the dispatcher.

Avoiding obvious questions about the weather to buy time, I asked, "Nice car, how does it drive?"

"Smooth . . . real smooth, sir,"

Not as smooth as his answers, I thought. One more 'sir' and was going to nominate him for mister congeniality award. Sam walked toward the squad car and whispered to me "the registered owner is a Kevin O'Donnell, but the car is clear, no report of it being stolen." Going out on limb and assuming the African American in my back seat is not Kevin O'Donnell, I gestured for Sam to get in the car. Turning to speak to the man I asked, "what's your name?"

"My name is Joe . . . Joe Jackson."

"Well Joe," I informed him, "that's not the name on the car registration."

Smiling as if he didn't have a care in the world, he replied, "the Secretary of State screwed up my registration before . . . you know . . . government bureaucracy."

He had a point there. The Secretary of State got my registration switched with another car awhile back and it was a nightmare trying to straighten it out. And since the car has not been reported stolen, it was looking like two strikes and Sam and I were out. Being stubborn, and knowing the car had to be stolen, I drove Mr. Jackson to the station under the pretext we had to check to see if he had a valid driver's license. Extending my arm to a bench inside the station door, "have a seat here," I said to Mr. Jackson, "this won't take long." I gathered more information from him to check the station computer for a valid license.

Meanwhile, Sam was out of sight talking to the dispatcher. The registered owner of the vehicle lived about 5 miles away and Sam asked the dispatcher to send a car to that address to verify if the registration was just a mix up. Our only hope was that the registered owner was home and, for some unknown reason, did not know his car was stolen.

Playing for more time, I imputed Mr. Jackson's information in the station computer and found a valid license. He checked out, with no warrants. Just as I began to doubt myself, an officer arrived at the station with a man at his side.

"This is Mr. Kevin O'Donnell," the officer informed me. The man was visibly upset and spoke with an Irish brogue that made him difficult to understand. While every other word out of his mouth was "bloody this" and "bloody that," Sam and I were able to piece together the following: Mr. O'Donnell was passing through our beat (first mistake) and stopped at a convenience store to grab a pack of cigarettes (second mistake). Figuring he would pop in and out he left the vehicle running (third mistake). When he got back the car was gone, and since he left the cell phone in the car, he couldn't call the police. He took a bus home and was walking up to the house when the officer arrived and asked about his car.

"Bingo," Sam broadcasted to me, "I knew it."

"You called it," I complimented Sam, "you can have the honors of arresting Mr. Jackson." Sam strolled over to the bench where Mr. Jackson was seated and said, "I got some good news and some bad news. The good news is the computer confirms you have a valid license, the bad news is you are under arrest for auto theft." Sam handcuffed the man and led him away.

I turned my attention back to Mr. McDonnell who shook my hand and thanked me for returning his car so quickly. He wanted to know how I found his car before he even reported it stolen.

"Well," I said, "I could lie to you and say it was because of years of experience or my finely honed police skills, but that would be a lie. Instead, it was your bumper sticker on the rear of the car. It's not often you see an African American driving a car with a bumper sticker that reads I LOVE IRISH FOLK MUSIC.

# CHAPTER 16

# The Holy Spirit

The beat Sam and I patrol is approximately 12 square blocks. Throughout the years we must have been up and down every street hundreds of times and been in every residential and commercial store multiple times on calls; but today was a first when the dispatcher called and Sam answered the radio. "Beat 3322 handle the disturbance at The First Blessed Church . . . see Father Ed." There are several storefront churches on our beat with self-proclaimed reverends—most of those seem more like a tax dodge than a legitimate church (Non-profits do not pay real estate taxes). But the First Blessed was a Catholic Church that sprawled across an entire city block. The structure was over 100 years old, carved from limestone with bell towers on two ends. It held services on Sunday and the congregation was mostly elderly parishioners.

Usually Sam takes his leisure driving to calls, but he picked up the pace for this one. "What could this be about?" Sam wondered out loud.

"Maybe it's a sign," I teased Sam, "it is Sunday and you haven't been to confession in years."

"You should talk, when was the last time you been to church?"

"It's been awhile, I have to confess . . . . see I just made a confession."

"Real funny," Sam said with a straight face. Sam parked in front of the church and we walked up to the front door. Sam pulled on the handle but the door was locked. "How can a church be closed on Sunday?"

I shrugged my shoulders. "Let's go around back." Sam opened a back door which lead directly into the priest's changing room off the altar. Peering out the door into church, I could see a priest sitting in a chair behind the altar table staring down at the pews. As big as the building looked from the outside, the inside was cavernous. Past the altar were several huge arches high above that travelled the length and width of the structure. Each arch was buttressed by two marble columns. About 100 people were scattered about the pews in silent prayer. Trying to get the priest's attention without disturbing anyone in the church I let out a low pitched "Pssssssst" sound. The priest arose from his chair and walked over to Sam and me. Closing the door behind him, he introduced himself, "I'm Father Ed . . . thank you for coming."

"A little trouble with the man upstairs?" Sam asked.

By the look in the priest's eyes I could see he wasn't in a laughing mood. His thoughts were definitely elsewhere as he struggled to find the words: "How shall I put this," he started, "the usher has informed me that a member of our church has stolen the offerings."

Trying to get a specific answer, I asked, "and by offerings, you mean . . .," dragging the sentence out waiting for a reply.

"500 bucks," he raised his voice, no longer being delicate.

"I'm sorry for you lose, Father, but what can the police do to help?"

"Get it back, of course."

I was speechless. I fixed my eyes over at Sam hoping he knew what to say. After an awkward moment of silence, Sam stated, "people who steal money don't hang around . . . I'm sure the thief is gone."

"No . . . no . . . no . . .," father Ed insisted, "the usher told me no one left the church and the doors are locked."

"Wait a minute," I said in disbelief, "all those people in the church are locked in?"

"Yes, I told the congregation what happened and that nobody was leaving until the guilty party returned the money."

Nothing like a little hostage taking to act as an incentive, I thought to myself. I didn't want to offend the priest but he had to be told you cannot detain people against their will. Trying to be as tactful as possible, I informed the priest, "Father, we can't line people up and start searching people . . . where would I start . . . with the nuns or the altar boys?"

"That's not what I had in mind . . . but maybe if you spoke to the congregation, reassuring the guilty party that he would not be arrested, the person might be persuaded to return the money."

I looked over at Sam who diverted his eyes away from me. I could tell he wanted no part of this either. I almost expected some host with a camera to jump out of a closet and tell me I was on some reality show. Was I really standing in the priest's chambers and being asked to take the pulpit to give a sermon? Avoiding the request for the moment, I asked the priest, "I would like to talk to the usher who reported the money missing."

Father Ed left the room to find the usher. "Quick," Sam stated, "let's get out of here."

As much as I wanted to make a break for it also, I reminded Sam "we can't run out on a priest."

"That would be some bad karma," Sam conceded, "but this is crazy. One hundred people are locked in a church and unlawfully detained—it is called false arrest. I can see the nightly news now with our mug shots on the screen and the caption—police arrest innocent victims attending church."

I reminded Sam, "we didn't lock them in . . . the priest did."

"If the news media gets a hold of this, who do you think they are going to portray as the bad guy . . . a catholic priest or the big, bad police? And think of the liability issue if someone decides to sue for false arrest. When he gets back tell him there's a separation of church and state issue and we can't get involved."

The door opened and father Ed returned with an elderly gentlemen. He appeared about 80 years old and shuffled his feet when he moved. He looked feeble and hunched forward a little. "This is Tom," father Ed informed us, "he collects the money and brings it to me after every mass."

So much for it being an inside job, I thought, the usher wouldn't have the strength to steal a feather. The usher went on to explain he collected about 500 dollars, mostly in crumpled singles, and emptied the money from the collection plate into a plastic bag. He put the collection plate away and when he returned the bag was ripped open and the money was gone. He walked to the altar and informed Father

Ed who instructed him to lock the doors. The usher, and Father Ed, do not recall anyone leaving the church before the doors were locked.

Making a pact with the priest (I guess that's better than making one with the devil) I informed Father Ed I would say a few words to the congregation if he promised to open the doors immediately thereafter; he agreed.

Before leaving the room, father Ed handed me a cruet and said "this might help." I took a swig of the wine and headed for the pulpit. The pulpit was a three-sided wooden box with an opening in the back. I walked up two steps to enter and gazed down upon the congregation. I could feel every eye upon me as I leaned forward to speak into the microphone. "Attention, good people," I began, "father Ed asked me to say a few words. I'm from the police department, and, first of all, I want to guarantee that whoever took the churches money will not be prosecuted. Second, being church-goers you should know there is an amendment about stealing."

Someone from the first row shouted, "you mean commandment."

"That's right . . . sounds like amendment though," I answered while touching my nose like in a game of charades. Standing in the pulpit a sense of power came over me as my voice was raised, "whoever took the money can remain anonymous . . . leave the money under the pew. Remember, vengeance is mine says the Lord." I had no idea what that had to do with stealing money but it did sound good and I was on a roll. "God knows all and sees all. He knows who stole the money." Just then the lights flickered and I thought I heard a clap of thunder from outside.

To my amazement, the congregation let out a collective "alleluia."

Then, I thought hit me, as I asked everyone to come forward from their pew and stand before the altar. Milling near the altar, I instructed everyone to join hands and say I silent prayer for the return of the money. While everyone joined hands and bowed their heads I left the pulpit and walked down to the crowd. I scanned the floor and saw a dollar bill crumpled on the floor next to an aging man. The man's body frame was thin but he had a noticeable bulge around the waist. Thinking fast, or filled with the Holy Spirit, it occurred to me whoever stole 500 dollars in crumpled bills could not fit that amount of money into a pocket. The person would have to stuff the money under a shirt to hide it. And if everyone was holding hands, that person couldn't hold the shirt closed to prevent the money from falling out. After the prayer ended, the usher flung open the doors and people started heading for the exits. The man with the bulge dropped several more bills from under his shirt, leaving a trailing as he walked. I marched quickly to the rear of the church and intercepted him before he reached the door. Putting a hand on his shoulder I said, "I would like to talk to you, sir."

"Me . . . I didn't do anything," he replied.

I looked down at his pant leg as another bill dropped to the floor. "Either you are molting or losing money," I informed him while pointing to the wrinkled bill by his foot.

The man started to cry. Father Ed and Sam joined us as the man admitted to taking the money. Looking weak and frail, the old gentlemen described how he was about to evicted from his apartment. His Social Security check barely covered his expenses and he came up short this month. It was food or rent, he couldn't afford both. Father Ed hugged the man and said, "everything is going to be fine . . . the church will look after you."

Sam and I have always made it a point to not get emotionally involved in our work. We see all kinds of pain and suffering, and staying emotionally unattached is our coping mechanism. But this one got to me. I reached into my pocket and pulled all I had—125 dollars. Sam ponied up 110 dollars. "Here . . . I hope this helps," I told Father Ed as I handed over the money.

"Bless you," Father Ed remarked as he walked the man up the aisle.

Sam and I walked out the church door feeling good—that doesn't happen very often. Outside, an elderly lady, with a warm smile and an angelic face, walked up and handed me a business card. It was from a law firm. "You'll be hearing from my attorney," she threatened.

# CHAPTER 17

# Courtroom drama

My cell phone began ringing at about 7:00 A.M. and wouldn't stop. My head was pounding and the stench of alcohol still permeated my breath from last night. Sam worked alone yesterday as I used a vacation day to attend a wedding. I had a marvelous time seeing my niece getting married. The firewater went down smooth yesterday and now it is payback. Answering the phone was the only way to stop it from ringing, "What," I blurted into the receiver.

"This is the desk sergeant . . . Your partner can't make court this morning so I'm notifying you . . . It's gun court-branch 55 at 8:00 A.M." He hung up the phone before I could protest. Before falling back into a comatose state I hit the speed dial number on the phone.

Sam answered "hello," his voicing cracking.

"The desk sergeant called . . . something about court this morning."

"Sorry partner. I arrested a suspect with a gun while you were enjoying yourself at the party last night. I added your name to the arrest report . . . I knew you would want credit for the arrest too. But this morning I woke up with the flu and been throwing up all morning. I called the desk sergeant to inform him I couldn't make court. It's only the preliminary hearing . . . one of us has to go or the case will be thrown out of court. Since the report has you listed as the second arresting officer, I need you to appear. The defendant's name is Franklin."

"You owe me," I forewarned Sam before dropping the phone to the floor. I stumbled to the bathroom, ran a wet comb through my hair and quickly shaved. My other uniforms were still at the cleaners so I was forced to wear the one from two days ago lying in the hamper. I tried to convince myself I did not look that bad as I stood in front of the full-length mirror. The shirt wrinkles were obvious and a spaghetti splotch over the left breast pocket looked like a bloodstain. I hopped in the car and arrived in the courtroom as the judge was calling the room to order. Sitting in the first row which is reserved for police officers I observed several officers to my right and left. Fortunately, several of my fellow officers worked the midnight shift and came directly to court from work. They had the I-need-sleep-look with disheveled clothing also.

The prosecutor for the state was a new face. I been to court often and never saw her before. She presented herself quite studious with wire framed glasses that were blue and matched her eyes. Her hair was pulled back tightly and swirled in a bun. She walked over to me and asked, "what case you on?"

"Franklin," I answered. The attorney, obviously taking pity on my appearance, decided to call my case first. It is common for the prosecuting attorney to show a preference for midnight officers—they know the officers worked all night and the last thing they wanted was to sit in court all day. The practice is similar to triage at an emergency room—the worst go first. Between my creased uniform and broken down appearance she assumed I just worked eight hours. With my hangover I was not about to set her I straight—I wanted to get home and collapse as soon as possible. The attorney groped through a stack of files on her desk and pulled one from the stack. Handing it me she said, "Franklin . . . you will be first on the docket."

The purpose of the preliminary hearing is to establish probable cause for the arrest. The defendant's name is called and he is escorted into the courtroom by a sheriff's deputy and presented to the judge. The arresting officer also approaches the bench and reads the arrest report into the court record. The judge listens to the testimony and says "finding of probable cause" in which case a court date is set for trial; or the judge decides "no finding of probable cause," in which case the defendant is free to go. The function of the hearing is to weed out cases where evidence is lacking before it gets to trial. In reality, it's just a rubber stamp—rarely is a case dismissed at a preliminary hearing.

I peeled open the brown vanilla file the attorney handed me and glanced at Sam's arrest report. The suspect, Franklin, was stopped for a traffic violation and a gun was found under the seat. He was charged with possession of a weapon—simple enough. I would read Sam's words into the court record to establish probable cause and Sam would appear for the trial at a later date.

A clerk of the court, standing next to the judge, stood up and yelled "Franklin." A door behind the judge's bench opened and a man in an orange jumpsuit was escorted into the courtroom by a deputy. The jumpsuit, stamped with DOC (Department of Corrections) on the back was standard attire for all prisoners. The defendant gazed at me with a "I don't remember you arresting me' expression.

The state's attorney nodded for me to come forward. I proceeded to step up to the bench and stood shoulder to shoulder with her. Out of the left corner of my eye I glanced at the video camera stationed on a tripod in the corner. All court proceedings are televised on a local public broadcasting station. There I stood looking folded, crimpled and mutilated.

Usually, I public defendant lawyer represents the defendant, but a tall man in a three piece black suit with a three-day beard and sunken eyes approached the bench and stood next to the defendant. Looking a lot more shady then his client he addressed the judge: "for the record, your honor, I'm Clyde Blake, attorney for the defendant."

"So entered," the judge replied.

The prosecuting attorney turned in my direction and started with the normal question such as name, badge number and unit of assignment. She finished with "calling your attention to June 5th, 10:20 P.M., can you describe what occurred?"

I peeked down at Sam's arrest report and answered: "On the date and time I stopped the defendant for a traffic violation and recovered a gun from under the seat of the vehicle."

The prosecuting attorney wrapped it up with "thank you, officer. Your honor, the state requests a finding of probable cause and requests a trial date."

I spun around on my heels to leave as the judge started to speak. "It is the finding of this court . . ."

91

"Your honor," the defense attorney interrupted, "I would like to ask the officer some questions?"

The judge ruled "go ahead."

I stopped in mid-spin and twisted my body back toward the bench. Suddenly my adrenaline kicked in and I was wide awake. I thought to myself, there are no questions at a preliminary hearing . . . how can I answer questions since I wasn't there? What could he possibly ask and how could I answer? Do I start making answers up? Whatever I say is taken down by a court reporter and can't be changed later. More importantly, lying in court is perjury. The old joke about 'I'm not here to testify but to testi-lie' didn't seem funny at the moment.

The defense attorney, looking cocky, asked, "how many people were in the car with the defendant when the car was stopped?"

It occurred to me where he was going with us. If other people were in the car with the defendant, how could it be proved it was the defendant's gun? Apparently there were other people in the car the defense attorney was trying to establish doubt as to who owned the gun. My mind was racing as I tried to formulate an answer. I was panic stricken. As I opened my mouth to speak, I made several gurgling noises but no words came out. A combination of my alcohol induced hangover and a sudden overpowering terror turned my face flush. I leaned forward to vomit as my stomach heaved and my throat constricted but nothing came up. Every eye in the courtroom, not to mention the video camera, locked onto me having the dry heaves. Still convulsing, I rotated my body away from the judge and hurried out the rear door into the corridor. Locating the men's bathroom across the way, I rushed in and locked the door behind me. The convulsions stopped and I began to breathe normal. Checking the wash area and stalls, I was relieved the bathroom was empty.

A loud knock on the door startled me. "Are you O.K. in there?" a voice I recognized as the prosecuting attorney asked through the door.

"I need a minute," I responded.

"The judge called a recess . . . take all the time you need."

Hearing her footsteps get softer, I reached for my cell phone and called Sam. As the phone rang I whispered, "please . . . please . . . answer the phone."

Finally, Sam said "hello."

"I'm in trouble here and need your help."

"I thought you were in court?"

"I am in court . . . and the defense attorney is asking me questions about a case I know nothing about."

Sounding surprised, Sam said, "no one asks questions at a preliminary hearing."

After banging the phone against the wall to get Sam's attention and let out my frustration, I sternly said, "the defendant has some slick attorney and he is asking questions . . . and I need answers . . . what the hell happened?"

Sensing my aggravation, Sam got serious. "I stopped the car for running a red light. Franklin was driving and there were two of his friends in the back seat. I arrested him for having a suspended license. When I searched the car I found the gun under the driver's seat where Franklin was sitting."

"Anything else I need to know?

"That is it," Sam assured me.

I disconnected the phone and walked back into the courtroom. As I took my seat the prosecuting attorney signaled me to approach the bench. The judge returned to the courtroom and looked at me with a sympathetic face and stated, "are you able to continue, officer?"

"Yes, your honor, I apologize. I think I have the flu."

The judge addressed the court reporter, "can you read back the question for the officer?"

The court reporter pulled the roll of paper from her machine and studied the little holes in the paper. She read out loud: "how many people were in the car with the defendant when the car was stopped?"

Feeling confident, I answered, "three occupants . . . two were in the backseat and the defendant was driving . . . and the gun was under the driver's seat."

The judge stopped the proceeding. "that is enough . . . finding of probable cause."

Completely embarrassed, I darted for the door without looking back. None of the officers in court with me were from my district so I figured I wouldn't get a ribbing at work, and nobody watches court TV, so I assumed the worst was over and I could forget about the incident.

Driving home my cell phone rang. I recognized Sam's number on the screen and answered the phone. I thought of cussing him out for putting me through that, but I just wanted to put the embarrassing incident behind me. "Hi Sam," I answered.

Trying to talk as he laughed, the words stumbled out, "heard you put on quite a show in court?"

"How would know that?" I asked, afraid of the answer.

"One of the officers from our watch called me . . . he said he watched you on court TV . . . said it was the most hilarious, sidesplitting dam thing he ever saw."

"Go ahead and have your laugh . . . that's the thanks I get for doing you a favor. I'm glad it's over.

"Not really," Sam explained, "he taped it on his DVR. He said he is sending it to the national TV show 'America's Funniest Home Videos.'"

# CHAPTER 18

# A guy and his girl

A light drizzle fell on the windshield of the squad car as Sam steered around the corner. Sam and I were having an argument about one of his girlfriends—Samantha. He introduced us a few days ago and we took an instant dislike to each other. Sam changes girlfriends more often then I change my socks and I knew it would blow over. Sam had his little ways of showing his displeasure with me every time we have an argument. Today, every time he made a right turn (which was often) he would cut it short and the right rear tire would hit the curb bouncing me in the passenger seat. It was killing my back and Sam knew it. The argument was put on the back burner when the dispatcher called: "Beat 3322 . . . we got an anonymous call of a man dragging a woman behind a building."

"10-4," I acknowledged. Looking over at Sam I said, "see if you can get there without making any right turns."

The address of the call is a large parcel of land with an abandoned factory. It used to be a tire factory, but the building was gutted years ago and old tires are scattered throughout the property. Midnight officers call the area 'the hole.' The term refers to places where officers can hide the squad car out of the public eye. Officers on midnights go there to catch some sleep.

Sam pulled up to the location and headed down a driveway that snaked toward the building. The driveway was filled with potholes and weeds sprouted high between the cracked concrete. Dodging craters Sam weaved up to the building. No sign of a vehicle or any life.

"Go around back," I directed Sam.

The road ended and Sam pushed the squad car into weeds about three feet high as the car bumped along. The unevenness of the ground caused the car to buck like a horse.

"If we get stuck in this we will need a crane to get out," Sam remarked.

"Keep moving," I warned Sam.

After about 100 yards, the car reached a small clearing and the kick from the car stopped and the suspension leveled out. Ahead was a red pick-up trucked parked with the passenger door open.

"This would be a perfect spot to dump a body," Sam said.

I got a bad feeling about this also as Sam eased the car to a halt. Exiting the squad car I pulled my weapon and walked slowly toward the truck. The passenger compartment looked empty but I couldn't be sure. With arms extended and both hands on my gun and my finger on the trigger, I reached the open door. The truck was empty. I quickly turned my attention, and weapon, to the bed of the truck. Stretching my neck to see over the side panel, the bed was empty also.

Sam came up from behind. 'Now what?"

Taking in the surrounding, we were completely encompassed by weeds taller than Sam and me. The only sight visible was a three story apartment building in the distant. A tenant from the building must have seen a body being dragged and called the police. Someone who owned the truck had to be in the brush somewhere, and what he was doing couldn't be good.

"Whoever is here didn't come for a picnic," I thought out loud. Turning toward Sam I added, "I guess we wait him out."

Sam and I returned to the car and backed up into the tall weeds far enough to conceal the squad car. About five minutes went by when we observed a man appear from the brush and step briskly in the direction of the pick-up truck. The framework of his body was stout; he was wearing a hooded sweatshirt with the hood up over his head.

"Now,' I shouted to Sam.

Sam put the car in gear and approached. The man glanced at us coming and then down at his feet as he kept walking. I had the door open and my gun out before Sam stopped the car. "Hey . . . come over here," I ordered the man.

The man looked up as if surprised and pointed at himself. He said "me?"

I said, "no . . . the guy behind you," in a sarcastic voice.

He turned to see if anyone else was behind him and threw up his hands as if confused. The man was of Hispanic descent and his eyes were bulging.

Sam brushed by me and threw him up against the side panel of the truck. He searched him from top to bottom and found nothing but a wallet. Sam asked, "what are you doing here?"

He replied "I'm lost. I was hoping to find a way out of here."

Sam look incensed. "yea . . . right . . . let's make this easy . . . where's the body?"

All of a sudden the man looked perplexed and said "No comprendo?"

Sam raised his voice in anger and said, "no comprendo . . . you just answered several questions in the perfect queen's English and all of a sudden you don't understand." Sam clutched the man by the throat with his left hand and clenched his fist with his right hand. Sam and I learned a long time ago if you hit someone make sure you leave no marks. You can't later deny hitting a suspect if he's standing there with a black eye. The stomach was the best place to land a punch without leaving any evidence.

"Take it easy," I told Sam. That apartment building in the distance worried me. If a tenant called because he saw a body being dragged, then the tenant can also see Sam hitting the suspect. Rule number one is never leave marks, and rule number two is make sure there are no witnesses. I don't know if it was the anticipation of a punch in the gut or the seriousness in Sam's eyes but the man pointed into the brush and said "over there." Sam put handcuffs on the suspect to prevent him from running. He eased back a few steps giving the man breathing room and demanded, "show us where."

The man hung his head in defeat and walked toward the brush. With Sam and me on his tail he zigzagged several times through the dense foliage until he reached the spot. Sam and I stared wonderingly with our mouths open. Lying at the man's feet was a blow-up doll. Not your standard this a toy doll, but an anatomically correct female doll—the kind used for immoral purposes. The doll was dingy and grimy with significant wear around the orifices. Apparently it served its purpose and the man wanted to dispose of it.

"That's disgusting," Sam lectured the man, "can't you find a real woman?"

The man did not answer and kept his head low to avoid eye contact. He stood there deflated (pun intended).

Sam removed the handcuffs and told the man to pick up doll. The man dragged the doll back into the clearing and ordered him to stand there. Sam and I walked back to the squad car to talk in private. "He may have committed several sins, but no crimes," I said.

"Just let him go?" He deserves some punishment," Sam said with a frustrated expression.

"Getting caught by the police in the middle of nowhere with a blow-up doll is punishment enough. On a disgrace scale of one to ten—that's a ten."

Sam came around to my way of thinking but ordered the man to take the doll with him. The man dragged the doll to his pick-up truck and propped her up in the passenger seat. The man got in and drove away.

As they were leaving, seeing the back of both heads in the rear window, I said, "don't they make a lovely couple?"

Sam slapped himself in the forehead, "that reminds me, I promised Samantha I would get two tickets for the theater.

"How the hell could this remind you of that'? I had to ask.

"She wants to see the musical 'guys and dolls.'"

# EPILOGUE

Being a police officer is like having a front row ticket to every show in town. The citizens we serve can certainly make one laugh, but the problems we face seem insurmountable—from the drug dealers who control their real estate to gang bangers who mark their turf like dogs, only gangs use graffiti instead of urine.

The stories told in this book are meant to give a glimpse into the profession of a police officer—the good and the bad. I can honestly say I did a lot of good work in my career and touched many lives in a positive way. Conversely, I made a lot of mistakes, but always with the best intentions. Being able to laugh at one self, and the public we encounter, is the best stress reduction therapy. But the toll has been immense. The occupation suffers from one of the highest rates of suicide, divorces, addiction to drugs and alcohol, and health related problems. The stress can be enormous at times and comes from all directions resulting in an 'us' versus 'them' mentality. The 'them' being an ungrateful public, a hostile news media and the police brass who do not support the troops. When the public needs help they call 911, but who can a police officer turn to for help. My partner and I lean on a good laugh.

So remember, the next time you get stopped by the police for a traffic violation, try a warm smile and a good joke. If it is me who stopped you, I can guarantee you won't get a ticket. Don't forget: be nice and be polite. After all, I'm the last line of defense—scary isn't it?

Made in the USA
Middletown, DE
14 July 2019